Janice VanCleave's

Constellations for Every Kid

Other Titles by Janice VanCleave

Science for Every Kid series
  Janice VanCleave's Astronomy for Every Kid
  Janice VanCleave's Biology for Every Kid
  Janice VanCleave's Chemistry for Every Kid
  Janice VanCleave's Dinosaurs for Every Kid
  Janice VanCleave's Earth Science for Every Kid
  Janice VanCleave's Ecology for Every Kid
  Janice VanCleave's Geography for Every Kid
  Janice VanCleave's Geometry for Every Kid
  Janice VanCleave's The Human Body for Every Kid
  Janice VanCleave's Math for Every Kid
  Janice VanCleave's Oceans for Every Kid
  Janice VanCleave's Physics for Every Kid

Spectacular Science Projects series
  Janice VanCleave's Animals
  Janice VanCleave's Earthquakes
  Janice VanCleave's Electricity
  Janice VanCleave's Gravity
  Janice VanCleave's Machines
  Janice VanCleave's Magnets
  Janice VanCleave's Microscopes and Magnifying Lenses
  Janice VanCleave's Molecules
  Janice VanCleave's Plants
  Janice VanCleave's Rocks and Minerals
  Janice VanCleave's Volcanoes
  Janice VanCleave's Weather

A+ Project series:
  A+ Projects in Biology
  A+ Projects in Chemistry

Also
  *Janice VanCleave's 200 Gooey, Slippery, Slimy, Weird, and Fun
    Experiments*
  *Janice VanCleave's 201 Awesome, Magical, Bizarre, and Incredible
    Experiments*
  *Janice VanCleave's 202 Oozing, Bubbling, Dripping, and Bouncing
    Experiments*
  Janice VanCleave's Guide to the Best Science Fair Projects

Play and Find Out series:
  Janice VanCleave's Play and Find Out about Science
  Janice VanCleave's Play and Find Out about Nature

Janice VanCleave's

Constellations for Every Kid

Easy Activities That Make Learning Science Fun

John Wiley & Sons, Inc.
New York • Chichester • Weinheim • Brisbane • Singapore • Toronto

Copyright © 1997 by Janice VanCleave
Published by John Wiley & Sons, Inc.
Illustrations © Laurel Aiello

The publisher and the author have made every reasonable effort to ensure that the experiments and activities in this book are safe when conducted as instructed but assume no responsibility for any damage caused or sustained while performing the experiments or activities in this book. Parents, guardians, and/or teachers should supervise young readers who undertake the experiments and activities in this book.

Library of Congress Cataloging-in-Publication Data:
VanCleave, Janice Pratt.
    Janice VanCleave's constellations for every kid : easy activities
that make learning science fun.
      p. cm. — (Science for every kid series)
    Includes index.
    Summary: Describes twenty of the most prominent constellations,
including the Big Dipper, Orion, and Cancer, explains how to locate
them, and provides instructions for related activities.
    ISBN 0-471-15981-6 (cloth : alk. paper). — ISBN 0-471-15979-4
(pbk. : alk. paper)
    1. Astronomy—Observer's manuals—Juvenile literature.
2. Constellations—Study and teaching—Activity programs—Juvenile
literatures. [1. Constellations. 2. Astronomy—Observers'
manuals.] I. Title. II. Series: VanCleave, Janice Pratt. Janice
VanCleave science for every kid series.
QB46.V363   1997
523.8'022'3—dc20   96-35309

It is with great pleasure that I dedicate this book to my husband. During my 26-year teaching career, he lovingly and patiently built science equipment for the experiments that I designed. While there was much experimenting in our home when I taught, there is even more now that I write professionally. We are able to share the wonders of science together as I write different books. We had such fun observing the constellations that we joined a local group of stargazers in the McLennan County Astronomy Club.

We are both looking forward to the research and writing of the next book, which is about nutrition. For a change, all of the experiments in the refrigerator will be edible. He is a jewel not to mind living in a house that sometimes is more like a science laboratory than a home. So, let me express my appreciation to the bright star in my life, my husband, Wade Russell VanCleave.

Acknowledgments

This book was written for stargazers of all ages and especially for the following, who offered encouragement by their interest in my writings:

Andrew and Holly Black; Whitney Cooper; David and Sarah Decker; Lauren, Ashley, and Christopher Humphrey; Sean, Jordan, Jacob, Jessica, and Drake Kaiser; Brittany and Marcus Lackey; Laura Field and Adelaide Roberts; Ron, Anne, Sarah, Benjamin, and Rebecca Skrabanek; Patrick Walker; Ashley and Kelly Wrinkle.

A special note of thanks to the encouragement that my grandchildren give me. May these stargazers always find God's creations wonderfully exciting: Kimberly, Jennifer, Russell David, and Davin VanCleave; Lauren and Lacey Russell.

Contents

viii   Contents

Introduction

This book is about groups of stars called constellations. The word *constellation* means "stars together." Early stargazers played a connect-the-dots game with the stars. They imagined lines between the stars that formed the shapes of animals—such as bears, dogs, a dragon, a lion, and a horse with wings—and of people, including a king, a queen, a damsel in distress, and her rescuing hero. Objects such as a cup, a scale, and large and small dippers are also among the sky-dot pictures.

The names of the constellations have been passed from one generation to the next and from one country to the next. Often the Latin names are still used. While the names of the constellations are the same, the stories about the constellations vary with different cultures.

This book will explain how to find many of the constellations in the sky. It will also guide you in discovering answers to questions about stars and other objects in the night sky, such as, What is the Milky Way? How far away are the stars? and Does everyone on Earth see the same stars each night?

The book is designed to teach facts, concepts, and problem-solving strategies. The exercises, experiments, and other activities were selected for their ability to be explained in basic terms with little complexity. One of the main objectives of the book is to present the *fun* of science.

How to Use This Book

Read each section slowly and follow all procedures carefully. You will learn best if each section is read in order, as there is some buildup of information as the book progresses. The format for each section is as follows:

- The chapter subtitle identifies the focus of the chapter.
- **What You Need to Know:** A definition and explanation of facts you need to understand.
- **Let's Think It Through:** Questions to be answered or situations to be solved using the information from What You Need to Know.
- **Answers:** Step-by-step instructions for answering the questions posed in Let's Think It Through.
- **Exercises:** To help you apply the facts you have learned.
- **Activity:** A project related to the facts represented.
- **Solutions to Exercises:** With a step-by-step explanation of the thought process.

In addition, this book contains:

- **Appendix A:** Star maps for each of the four seasons.
- **Appendix B:** An alphabetical list and pronunciations of the constellations studied in this book.
- **Appendix C:** An alphabetical list and pronunciations of the stars studied in this book along with the constellation they appear in.
- A **Glossary:** The first time a term is introduced in the book, it will be **boldfaced** and defined in the text. The term and definition are also included in the Glossary at the end of the book. Be sure to flip back to the Glossary as often as you need to, making each term part of your personal vocabulary.

General Instructions for the Exercises

1. Read the exercise carefully. If you are not sure of the answers, reread What You Need to Know for clues.

2. Check your answers against those in the Solutions and evaluate your work.

3. Do the exercise again if any of your answers is incorrect.

General Instructions for the Activities

1. Read the activity completely before starting.

2. Collect all supplies. You will have less frustration and more fun if all the materials necessary for the activity are ready before you start. You lose your train of thought when you have to stop and search for supplies.

3. Do not rush through the activity. Follow each step very carefully; never skip steps, and do not add your own. Safety is of the utmost importance, and by reading each activity before starting, then following the instructions exactly, you can feel confident that no unexpected results will occur.

4. Observe. If your results are not the same as those described in the activity, carefully reread the instructions and start over from step 1.

How to Use the Star Maps

Star maps are used to locate constellations. Only the brighter stars are shown on the maps in this book. These maps show only the constellations discussed, not all of the visible constellations. See Appendix A for a more complete star map of each season. Appendix B provides an alphabetical list and pronunciations of the constellations studied in this book. Appendix C provides a comparable list of stars.

Five-pointed stars and circles are used to indicate stars. Dashed lines are shown between the stars in each constellation to depict the figure imagined by early stargazers. The name of the constellation and some of the stars are identified on the map. The direction indicated at the bottom of the map is the direction you are to face to see the stars in the position shown.

Since the sky looks different at different latitudes, one latitude, 40°N, has been chosen for the descriptions of constellation locations for all the maps. (Latitude is explained in chapter 2.) If you live north of this latitude, you will be able to see stars near the northern horizon that are not shown on the maps, and the stars near the southern horizon on the map will be nearer the horizon or below it and therefore out of sight. If you live south of the latitude, the reverse is true: Stars near the northern horizon on the map will be closer to the horizon or below it and out of sight, and stars not shown on the map will be visible. The maps are most useful within the continental United States and other areas between latitudes 25°N and 50°N.

For latitude 40°N, the constellations will be located in the general positions shown on the sky maps for the date and time shown. The time is Standard Time. Constellations that are visible at 10 P.M. Eastern Standard Time on February 1 will generally be in the same position shown at 10 P.M. Central Standard Time. While the time is the same throughout any one zone, the position of the constellations viewed by observers across the zone at that time is not the same. The stars appear as shown on the map from the central longitude of your time zone, but if you are west of center within your time zone, the constellations in the sky will be slightly eastward from the position shown on the star map. If you are east of center within your time zone, the constellations in the sky will be slightly westward from the position shown on the star map. To find the constellations at an earlier time than shown on the map, look more toward the east. For a later time, look more toward the west. For more information about constellation movement and using the star maps for earlier or later dates, see chapter 4, "Star Finder."

A flat map of the entire sky looks like a cross with four equal arms, the sides of which curve outward. Each arm on the map shows one of the four compass directions: north, south, east, or west. The outer end of each arm represents the horizon and has the words FACING NORTH, FACING SOUTH, and so on, to help you know how the map corresponds to the sky. If the map has FACING SOUTH at the bottom, then face south so that the map corresponds to the sky. In the center of the map, where all the arms converge, is a point directly overhead called the **zenith,** which is marked with an X.

The key to studying constellations is to have a clear, dark sky and a little patience. It may take a few minutes to find each constellation the first time, so take your time and get comfortable. A lawn chair or blanket will allow you to relax and leisurely gaze at the sky. After finding the known constellations, look for your own patterns in the sky and then make up stories to go with them.

1
Night Lights
Examining the Lights in the Nighttime Sky

What You Need to Know

Thousands of years ago, people told stories about the stars. They imagined lines between various stars so that groups of stars took on different shapes that represented people and objects in stories. These stories were passed from generation to generation. The stories may have changed with time, but the star groupings in the sky are generally the same. The figures that early stargazers imagined among the stars are now called **constellations** (groups of stars that appear to make patterns in the sky). There are 88 universally recognized constellations. Only at Earth's **equator** (an imaginary line that circles the center of Earth in an east-west direction) can most of the constellations be seen. But even at the equator you cannot see them all at once. This is because Earth blocks your view of part of the sky.

On any clear, dark night, you can see a hazy band of starlight across the night sky. This cloudy looking band stretches from one end of the horizon to the other. The ancient Greeks named this band of light the **Milky Way** because it looked like a trail of spilled milk across the sky. If you look closely at the Milky Way, you'll see dark streaks through it. This is the Great Rift, a chainlike system of large **nebulae** (clouds of gas and dust spread across many millions of miles [kilometers] in space). The Great Rift is an example of **dark nebulae,** since they do not give off visible light and are so thick that they partially or completely block the light from the stars behind them.

The Milky Way runs through the **Milky Way Galaxy.** A **galaxy** is an enormous group of stars, dust, and gas all held together by **gravity** (the force of attraction between celestial bodies that pulls them toward each other). The word *galaxy* comes from the Greek word for milk, *gala*.

The Milky Way Galaxy viewed from above would look like a spinning pinwheel, and from the side it would look flat and disk-like, much like a CD with a swollen center. Galaxies of this shape are called **spiral galaxies.** They have a bright, dense center and radiating arms of stars, planets, and other celestial bodies. The entire Milky Way Galaxy is spinning around its center in space. Our solar system lies within one of the spiral arms and is speeding around the center of the galaxy at about 563,000 miles per hour (900,800 kph). It takes about 200 million years for the solar system to make one complete trip.

The stars that make up constellations do not really have a five-pointed shape as they do in many pictures. **Stars** are actually gigantic spheres made mostly of hydrogen and helium gases. The centers of stars are very **dense** (having materials that are close together) and hot. The high temperatures cause the **atoms** (the smallest building blocks of matter) to move so fast that **nuclei** (centers of atoms) fuse, or join, when they collide, forming one nucleus. In a series of steps, four hydrogen nuclei fuse into one massive nucleus of helium and release a great amount of heat and light energy. This process is called **nuclear fusion.**

Stars, suns, moons, and planets are called **celestial bodies. (Celestial** means having to do with the sky.) Large celestial bodies that **revolve** (move around a central point) around a sun are called **planets.** A group of celestial bodies traveling around a star is called a **solar system,** and the star in the center is called a **sun.** Earth's sun is the brightest and closest star to Earth. The Sun and stars shine continuously, but the Sun is seen only dur-

ing the day and the stars are generally seen only at night. During the daytime, the light from the Sun is so bright that the light from stars is not noticeable.

During the nighttime, the sun is hidden below the earth's **horizon** (the line where the sky seems to meet Earth). While the Sun itself is hidden from view, its light can still be seen. This is because the Sun's light **reflects** (bounces back) off the surfaces of the Moon and the planets. (A **moon** is a small celestial body that revolves around a planet.) The Moon, which is the brightest light in the nighttime sky, actually reflects sunlight. The Sun and other stars are **luminous** (shine by their own light), but the Moon and the planets are not. The Moon and some planets shine only because they reflect light from the Sun.

Space between celestial bodies is mostly dark and practically empty. The **interstellar material** (material between celestial bodies) is about 99 percent gases, most of which is hydrogen, and 1 percent interstellar dust. This dust is not the type found around the house. House dust is mostly tiny particles of cloth, dirt, and dead skin cells. **Interstellar dust** is made of microscopic particles thought to be mainly carbon and/or silicates. (Sand is made of silicates.)

Let's Think It Through

Which figure—A or B—shows a star as a sun?

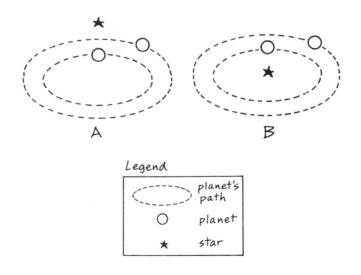

Answers

Think!

• A sun is a star that planets revolve around.

Figure B shows a star as a sun.

Exercises

1. Which figure—A or B—represents a constellation?

A   B

2. Which observer on Earth—A or B—is not able to see starlight because of the brightness of the Sun?

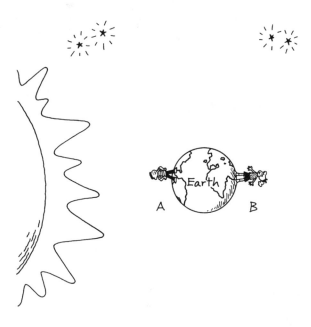

Activity: MOONLIGHT

Purpose   To distinguish between luminous and
nonluminous celestial bodies.

Materials   4-inch (10-cm) -square piece of aluminum foil
transparent tape
4-inch (10-cm) piece of string
large shoe box with lid
ruler
scissors
flashlight

Procedure

1. Crumple the aluminum foil into a grape-size ball.

2. Tape one end of the string to the aluminum ball.

3. Turn the shoe-box lid upside down, and tape the free end of
the string about 2 inches (5 cm) from the corner as shown so
that the string is parallel to the long sides of the lid.

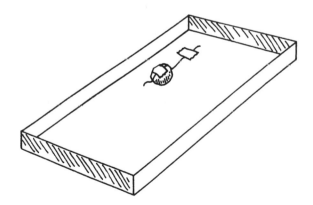

4. Cut a ½-by-2-inch (1.25-by-5-cm) flap about 2 inches (5 cm)
from the right corner of one short side of the box. Cut a 1-by-
2-inch (2.5-by-5-cm) flap about 1 inch from the opposite corner of the same side.

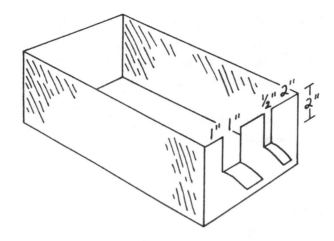

5. Close the large flap and place the lid on the box so that the ball hangs at the opposite end from the small, open flap.

6. Set the box on a table and look through the open flap toward the ball. Make note of the visibility of the hanging ball.

7. Raise the lid and open the large flap.

8. Repeat steps 5 and 6, shining the flashlight through the open flap toward the hanging ball inside the box.

Results   The aluminum ball is not visible or only slightly visible without the light from the flashlight. With the light from the flashlight, the ball appears shiny.

Why?   In this experiment, the ball represents the Moon, and the flashlight, the Sun. The Moon, like the model, is not luminous. The Moon shines only when light from a luminous celestial body, the Sun, reflects off of it.

Solutions to Exercises

1. *Think!*

   • A constellation is a group of stars that appears to make a pattern in the sky when the stars are joined by imaginary lines.

   Figure A is a constellation.

2. *Think!*

   • The Sun and the stars shine continuously, day and night, but during the daytime, the light from the Sun is so bright that the light from the stars is not noticeable.

   • Which observer is on the sunny side of Earth?

   Observer A cannot see starlight because of the brightness of the Sun.

2
Sky Address

Using a Celestial Sphere to Locate Places and Stars

What You Need to Know

Astronomers have designed an imaginary sphere to help locate celestial objects. Earth is pictured at the center of this large, hollow, rotating sphere with all other celestial bodies stuck on its inside surface. This imaginary picture of the sky is called the **celestial sphere.** (See chapter 11 for information about how the celestial sphere is used to plot the movement of the sun and constellations during the year.)

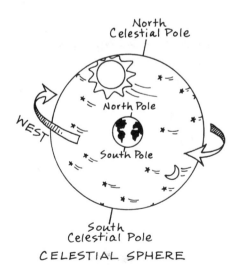

CELESTIAL SPHERE

Imaginary lines of reference on the sphere are used to locate stars and other celestial bodies, just as imaginary lines of reference are used to locate places on earth. A model of the earth with its reference lines is called a **terrestrial globe,** and a model of the celestial sphere with its reference lines is called a **celestial globe.**

Latitude and longitude lines are imaginary lines that circle Earth and are used to locate places on Earth. On a terrestrial globe, **latitude lines,** also called **parallels,** circle Earth parallel to its equator. They mark locations in degrees (°) north and south of the equator, which is at 0° latitude. **Longitude lines,** also called **meridians,** run from the **North Pole** to the **South Pole** (the northernmost and southernmost points on Earth, respectively). They mark locations in degrees east and west of the **prime meridian** (0° longitude that runs through Greenwich, England).

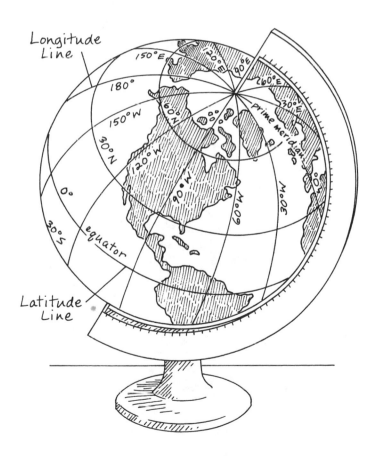

The imaginary lines on the celestial sphere are known as declinations and hour circles. A celestial body's **declination** is its position in degrees north or south of the **celestial equator** (an imaginary line at 0° declination that circles the celestial sphere.) The celestial equator is the same distance from the **north** and **south celestial poles,** which are above the North and South Poles of Earth. A positive declination, such as +60°, indicates a position north of the celestial equator. A negative declination, such as –60°, indicates a position south of the celestial equator.

A **great circle** is an imaginary circle on a sphere with the center point of the circle and the center point of the sphere being the same. An **hour circle** is a great circle passing through the north and south poles on the celestial sphere. (Half of such a circle from pole to pole passing through a celestial body is called its hour circle.) There is no limit to the number of hour circles that can be drawn. The hour circle that passes through the zenith and the north and south endpoints of an observer's

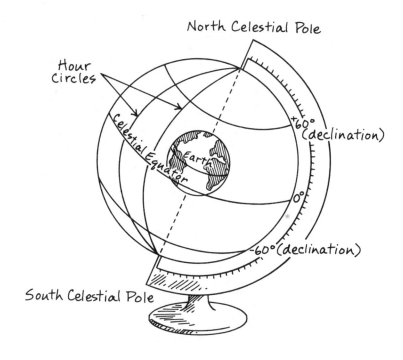

horizon is called a **celestial meridian.** Only half of the celestial meridian is above the horizon.

The east-west position of a celestial body is called its **right ascension** (the distance eastward from a zero-point). The zero-point, or starting point, for right ascension is the hour circle that passes through the vernal equinox. (The **vernal equinox,** or **spring equinox,** is the position of the Sun on or about March 21, when it crosses the celestial equator and heads north.) The right ascension of a celestial body is measured from the vernal equinox to the point where the body's hour circle crosses the celestial equator. Right ascension is usually measured in hours (^{h}), with 1 hour equaling 15°. In the diagram, the vernal equinox is the zero-point at 0^h. All the stars on circle 1 are on the same hour circle and have the same right ascension of 2^h but different declinations. The stars on circle 2 are on different hour circles and have different right ascensions, but all have the

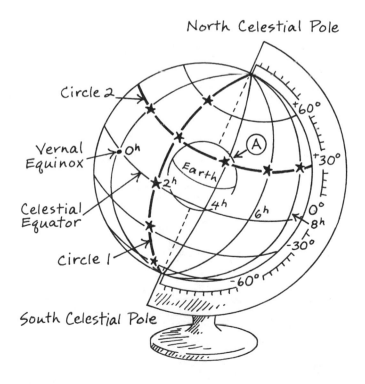

same declination of +30°. The **coordinates** (two numbers that mark the location of a place) of star A on the celestial sphere are written 4^h, +30°. As seen from Earth, every star has coordinates on the celestial sphere. These coordinates change very little from year to year and can be found on a celestial globe, in a star atlas, or in astronomy books such as on page 14 of *Astronomy,* by Dinah Moché (New York: Wiley, 1993).

Let's Think It Through

Use the celestial globe diagram to answer the following questions:

1. What are the coordinates for star A?

2. Which star has the coordinates 6^h, +30°?

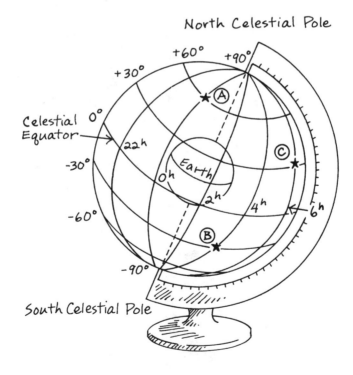

Answers

1. *Think!*

   - Find star A on the globe.

   - What is the right ascension of the hour circle passing through the star? 0^h

   - Which declination line is the star on?   +60°

   The coordinates of star A are 0^h, +60°.

2. *Think!*

   - Right ascension is measured in hours (^{h}). The right ascension coordinate is 6^h. Find 6^h on the globe.

   - Declination is measured in degrees (°). The declination coordinate is +30°. Find +30° on the globe.

   - Use your finger to trace the hour circle with the right ascension 6^h from the celestial equator to the declination line for +30°.

   Star C has the coordinates 6^h, +30°.

Exercises

1. Use the celestial globe diagram to identify the star with the coordinates 12^h, +60°.

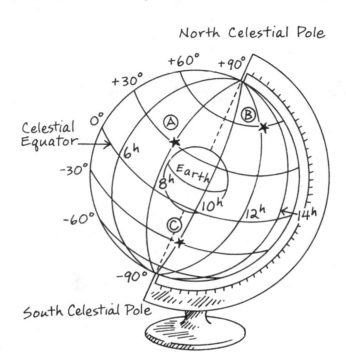

2. Study the diagram and determine which line—A or B—is the observer's celestial meridian.

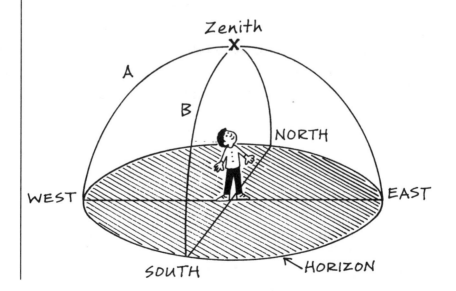

Activity: SKY GLOBE

Purpose To determine the coordinates of a star.

Materials masking tape
2-quart (2-liter) transparent bowl
marking pen
lemon-size ball of modeling clay
12-inch (30-cm) string

Procedure

1. Stick a piece of tape across the outside sides of the bowl from rim to rim so that the tape divides the bowl in half.

2. Stick a second piece of tape across the bowl, dividing the outside of the bowl into four equal parts.

3. Stick a third piece of tape around the outside rim of the bowl.

4. Mark a dot on the tape where pieces 1 and 2 cross. Label this dot +90°.

5. Mark three evenly spaced dots on each quarter section of tape, from the rim toward the center dot.

6. Starting at the rim of the bowl, label the first dot on each section of tape 0°, the second +30°, and the third +60°.

7. Starting where the tape around the rim of the bowl overlaps one quarter section, place eight evenly spaced dots along the tape on the rim. Label the dot at one of the 0° marks 0^h. Label the next dot to the right 3^h, and each successive dot an additional 3^h. The last label should be 21^h.

8. Tape one end of the string at the 90° mark on the top of the inverted bowl.

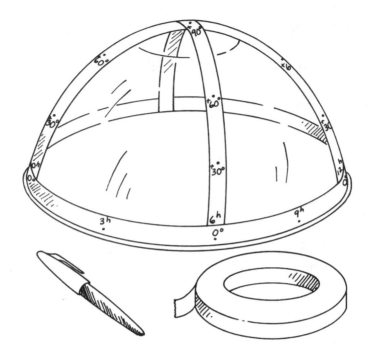

9. Shape the clay into a ball, then gently hit one side of the ball against a flat surface several times to flatten the side until the ball looks like half a ball. The clay ball represents half the Earth.

10. Place the clay Earth on a table and position the bowl over it so that the clay Earth is in the center of the area under the bowl.

11. Place a piece of tape on the side of the bowl above the 3^h mark and at a height level with the 30° mark.

12. Draw a star on the tape.

13. Position the string across the side of the bowl so that it crosses the star.

Results   The string crosses the 3^h mark on the rim of the bowl, and the star is the same height from the bowl's rim as the 30° mark.

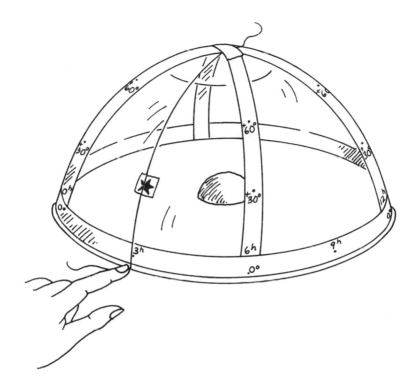

Why?   The bowl is a model of the northern part of a celestial globe. The tape around the rim of the bowl represents the celestial equator. The numbered dots around the rim mark right ascension locations, and the numbered dots on the quarter sections of tape mark declination locations. Since the numbers are positive, they are north of (above) the celestial equator. The string represents an hour circle. The coordinates of the star are $3^h, +30°$.

Solutions to Exercises

1.   *Think!*

> • The right ascension coordinate is 12^h. Find 12^h on the celestial equator.

- The declination coordinate is +60°. Find +60° on the globe.

- Use your finger to trace the hour circle for right ascension 12^h from the celestial equator to the declination line for +60°.

Star B has the coordinates 12^h, +60°.

2.   *Think!*

- An observer's celestial meridian is an hour circle passing through the zenith and the north and south endpoints of the observer's horizon.

Line B is the observer's celestial meridian.

3
Changing Sky

Determining Visible Constellations at Different Locations

What You Need to Know

On a clear, moonless night away from city lights, about 2,000 stars can be seen with the naked eye. If the moon is visible, or if other lights, such as streetlights or lights from homes are visible, only the brightest stars can be seen. Not all of the visible stars can be seen at once, because only part of the sky can be seen from any one place on Earth.

Most of the stars, the Sun, and the Moon appear to rise daily above the horizon in the eastern sky and set below the horizon in the western sky. Actually, none of these celestial bodies are moving across the sky. Instead, Earth is moving. The earth **rotates** (turns) on its **axis** (an imaginary line through the center of an object) once in about 23 hours and 56 minutes. This movement causes the stars to appear to move overhead.

The exit points of Earth's axis are called the South and North Poles. The South Pole is in the **Southern Hemisphere** (the region south of the equator) and the North Pole is in the **Northern Hemisphere** (the region north of the equator). The end of the axis at the South Pole points in the general direction of a constellation called **Corona Australis** (kuh-ROH-nuh aw-STRAY-lus). Because its star pattern resembles a cross, this constellation is often called the Southern Cross. The end of the axis at the North Pole points very close to a star called **Polaris** (puh-LAIR-us), or the **North Star.** Polaris is in the constella-

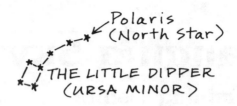

Polaris
(North Star)

THE LITTLE DIPPER
(URSA MINOR)

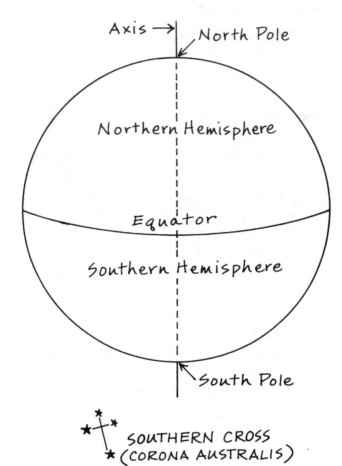

Axis → | North Pole

Northern Hemisphere

Equator

Southern Hemisphere

South Pole

SOUTHERN CROSS
(CORONA AUSTRALIS)

tion **Ursa Minor** (UR-suh MY-nur). The name *Ursa Minor* means "Little Bear," but the constellation is more commonly known as the Little Dipper. Constellations that are always above the horizon from a given location on Earth are called **circumpolar constellations.** These constellations never set but simply go round and round the celestial poles without dipping below the horizon. From the North Pole, all Northern Hemisphere constellations are circumpolar. From the equator, there are no circumpolar constellations.

The stars that you see in the sky depend on where you are on Earth. When you look at the sky at night, you see only the stars that are above the horizon. These are about half of the stars that are visible to the naked eye from your location. Below the horizon is another set of stars. These stars are hidden from view because Earth blocks your view. Thus, the combination of stars seen at the North Pole is different from that seen at 40 degrees north latitude (40°N) or at the South Pole on the same night.

Earth's movements also affect the stars you see. Earth not only rotates but also changes position in the sky as it revolves around the Sun. Earth's movement around the Sun causes a slight change in the part of the celestial sphere seen each night. This results in different parts of the celestial sphere being visible during each season.

Let's Think It Through

In the diagram on the next page, Jennifer and Kimberly are observing the celestial sphere from different locations. Jennifer is closer to the North Pole. Study the diagram and answer the following:

1. Which observer(s) is located in the Southern Hemisphere?

2. Which area—A or D—is closer to the constellation Corona Australis?

3. Which area—A, B, C, or D—contains constellations not visible to either Jennifer or Kimberly?

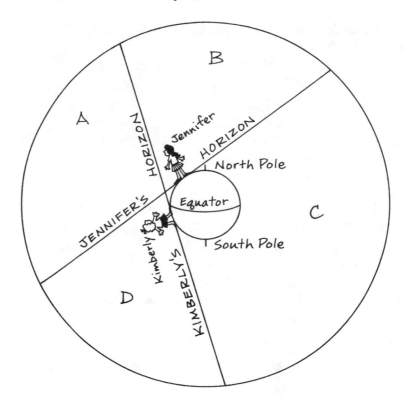

Answers

1.   *Think!*

- The Southern Hemisphere is the region of Earth below the equator.

  Kimberly is located in the Southern Hemisphere.

2.   *Think!*

- The South Pole of Earth points in the general direction of Corona Australis, the Southern Cross.

  Region D is closer to the constellation the Southern Cross.

3. *Think!*

- Constellations below the horizon are not visible.

- Which region is below the horizons of both Jennifer and Kimberly?

Region C is not visible to either Jennifer or Kimberly.

Exercises

The diagram shows two sky observers on Earth. David is located at a latitude closer to the equator and Lacey is at a latitude closer to the North Pole. Study the diagram and answer the following:

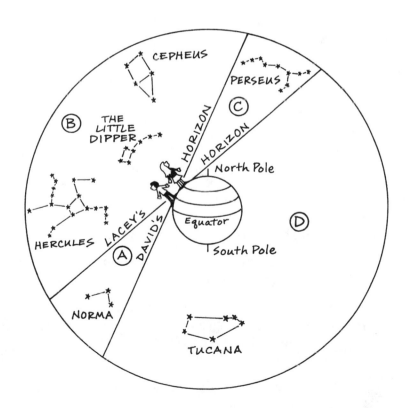

1. Which constellations are visible to David but not to Lacey?

2. Which constellations are visible to both David and Lacey?

3. Which constellations are not visible to either David or Lacey?

Activity: STAR DISK

Purpose To create and use an instrument that shows which constellations are visible to observers at different latitudes.

Materials marking pen
5-by-5-inch (12.5-by-12.5-cm) tracing paper
ruler
3-by-5-inch (7.5-by-12.5-cm) index card
scissors
one-hole paper punch
paper brad

Procedure

1. Trace the Mock Celestial Sphere pattern onto the paper. *NOTE: Place the lettered areas in the diagram exactly as shown.*

2. Use the ruler to draw a line straight across the index card starting ½ inch (0.63 cm) from one of the long sides.

3. In the center of the line draw a pointer with a stick-figure observer as in the diagram.

4. Cut along the line and around the pointer. Discard the two cutaway pieces.

5. Use the paper punch to make a hole below the base of the pointer.

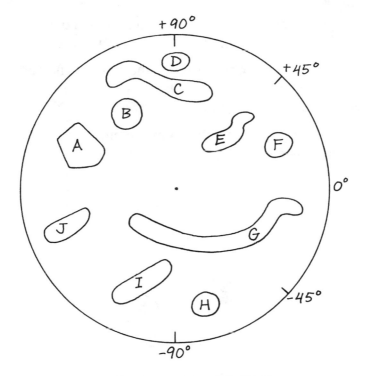

MOCK CELESTIAL SPHERE

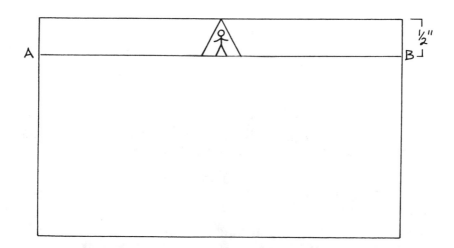

6. Place the card over the tracing so that the hole in the card aligns with the dot in the center of the tracing.

7. Insert the paper brad through the hole in the card, then punch the brad through the dot in the center of the tracing. Secure the brad.

8. Rotate the card so that the pointer points to +90° on the celestial sphere.

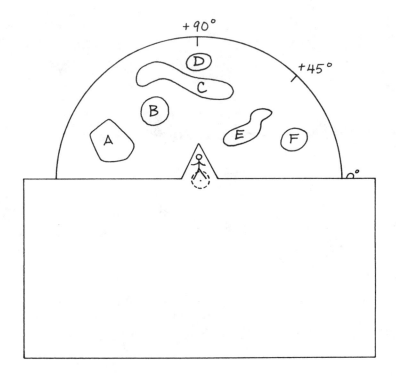

9. Make note of the lettered areas that are visible on the tracing. These represent the constellations of the celestial sphere that are visible above the horizon.

10. Repeat steps 8 and 9, moving the pointer to +45°, 0°, – 45°, and –90°.

Results   The visible constellations are different depending on where the pointer is set.

Why?   The point on the celestial sphere directly above the observer (the stick figure on the pointer) is the zenith. When the observer is at latitude 90°N on Earth, the zenith is declination +90° on the celestial sphere. The group of visible constellations from this latitude is different from those for observers at other latitudes. Different positions of the pointer represent different latitudes for observers on Earth. At different latitudes, the zenith and horizon change. For example, when the observer's zenith is at +90°, the constellations seen are A through F. At −45°, constellations F, H, I, and part of G are visible. Thus, the nighttime sky looks different from different latitudes.

Solutions to Exercises

1.   *Think!*

- An observer can see the stars above the horizon.

- Which constellations are above David's horizon but not above Lacey's?

  *David can see constellation **Norma** (NOR-muh), the Level, but Lacey cannot.*

2.   *Think!*

- What part of the celestial sphere is above both David's and Lacey's horizons? Region B.

- What constellations are in region B?

  ***Hercules** (HUR-kyoo-leez), the Kneeler; **Cepheus** (SEE-fyus), the King; and the Little Dipper are visible to both David and Lacey.*

3. *Think!*

- Constellations below the horizon are not visible.

- Which region is below the horizon of both David and Lacey? Region D.

- What constellation is in region D?

Tucana (too-KAN-uh), the Toucan, is not visible to either David or Lacey.

4
Star Finder

Using a Star Map to Find Constellations

What You Need to Know

Before actually looking for constellations in the sky, it helps to know how to measure the apparent space between the stars. Your hands can be used as a guide. These measurements are rough and depend greatly on arm length and hand size. They have nothing to do with the real distances between the stars, but they can be used to find constellations and to direct others to the location of constellations.

First, hold your left arm straight out in front of you. Point your little finger up toward the sky. Close one eye and look at your little finger. The width of your little finger measures about 1° of the sky. Now point your first three fingers upward. They measure about 5° of the sky. Your fist measures about 10°. If you raise and spread your index and little fingers, the space measured between them is about 15°. Now raise and spread your thumb and little finger. The space measured between them is about 25°. The diagram shows the degrees measured by each of these hand positions.

From day to day and from hour to hour, the constellations in the sky appear to move. On a star map, this movement is in a counterclockwise direction around Polaris. A single constellation moves about 361° every 24 hours. There are 360° in a circle. This extra degree of constellation movement adds up to about

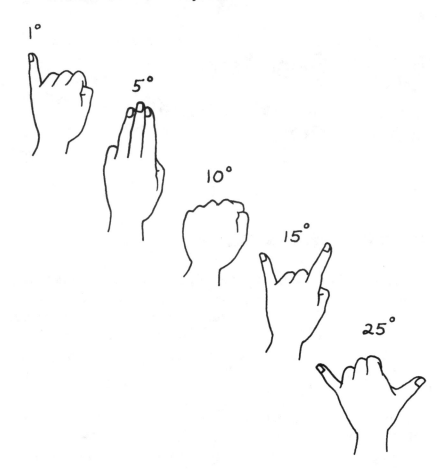

30° a month. So a constellation's position at 8:00 P.M. on June 1 is 30° to the right (to the west if facing south) of that shown on a star map for 8:00 P.M. on May 1, and at 8:00 P.M. on April 1 it was 30° to the left (to the east if facing south) of the position shown on the May star map.

There are two ways to use the star maps in this book. One way is to stand outdoors facing the compass direction indicated at the bottom of the map. Hold the map above your head so that the map is facing downward with the bottom of the map pointing in the direction you are facing. This position allows you to

look up at the map and compare it with the star patterns in the sky. To see the map easily without affecting your **night vision** (ability to see in the dark), you should use an astronomer's flashlight to light the map. (See the activity in this chapter for instructions on constructing this kind of light.)

Another way to use a star map is to stand outside facing the direction indicated at the bottom of the map. Hold the map in front of you so that the bottom of the map faces you. Adjust the height and angle until the map is easy to read. The constellations at the bottom of the map will be found near the horizon you are facing.

Let's Think It Through

The Big Dipper is an **asterism** (a group of stars with a shape within a constellation) within **Ursa Major** (UR-suh MAY-jur), the Great Bear. The diagrams and star maps in this book show only the Big Dipper, not all of Ursa Major. Study the diagrams on the next page and answer the following:

1. How many degrees is it from the end star in the Big Dipper's handle to the outermost star in its bowl?

2. How many degrees is it between the two outer stars in the Big Dipper's bowl?

THE BIG DIPPER

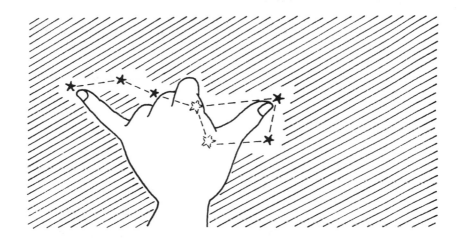

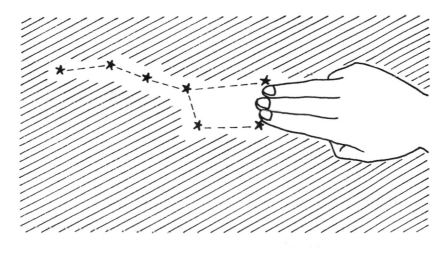

Answers

1. *Think!*

    • What part of the hand shown is being used to measure
    the distance from the end of the Big Dipper's handle to
    the front of its bowl? The little finger and thumb when
    they are spread apart.

    • How many degrees is it between the little finger and
    thumb when they are spread apart?

    *It is about 25° from the end star in the Big Dipper's han-
    dle to the outermost star in its bowl.*

2. *Think!*

    • What part of the hand shown is being used to measure
    the distance between the two outer stars in the Big Dip-
    per's bowl? The first three fingers.

    • The width of the first three fingers is equal to how many
    degrees?

    *It is about 5° between the two outer stars in the Big Dip-
    per's bowl.*

Exercises

1. Study the diagram and determine how many degrees the
    lowest star is above the horizon.

2. Study the star map and answer these questions:

    a. Which constellation is closest to the southernmost part
    of the horizon?

    b. In what general direction would you look to find the
    constellations on March 1 at 10:00 P.M.?

c. If the sky is being observed on February 1 at 9:00 P.M., in what general direction would each of the constellations be found?

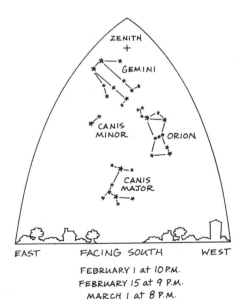

Activity: LIGHT OUT

Purpose   To construct an astronomer's flashlight.

Materials   ruler
scissors
red transparent report folder
flashlight
rubber band

Procedure

1. Cut a 4-by-8-inch (10-by-20-cm) strip from the red folder.

2. Fold the strip in half to form a 4-inch (10-cm) square.

3. Cover the end of the flashlight with the square and secure with the rubber band.

4. Use the flashlight to read star maps outdoors at night.

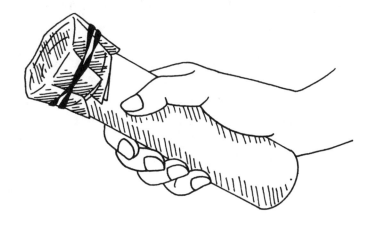

Results   An astronomer's flashlight is constructed.

Why?   When you move from a lighted area to a dark area, at first you can hardly see. After a few minutes, changes occur in your eyes and you see better. In about 30 minutes to 1 hour, the changes are complete and your vision is even better. Although your vision is not as good as in the light, it is the best it will be in the dark. You now have night vision.

One flash of white light can reverse the changes in the eye, causing you to lose your night vision. It takes another 30 to 60 minutes or so to get it back again. Red light affects night vision less than does white light, so the astronomer's flashlight is covered with a red filter. You can read your star map with the red light and still see the stars in the sky.

Solutions to Exercises

1. *Think!*

- How many degrees wide is the fist? About 10°.
- How many fists above the horizon is the star? Four.
- Four fists equals how many degrees? 4 × 10 = ?

  The star is about 40° above the horizon.

2a. *Think!*

- Where is the southernmost part of the horizon? At the bottom of the map near the side marked *facing south*.
- Which constellation is closest to the bottom of the map?

  Canis Major *(KAY-nus MAY-jur), the Great Dog, is closest to the southernmost part of the horizon on the map.*

b. *Think!*

- Each month, constellations move counterclockwise 30° from the previous month's position at the same time.

- This counterclockwise movement is toward the right on the star map.

- Facing south, what compass direction is to the right on the star map?

  On March 1 at 10:00 P.M., the constellations are located to the right, or west, of the positions shown on the star map.

c. *Think!*

- Each hour, constellations move about 15°.

- This movement is toward the right on the star map.

- At an earlier hour, the position of the constellations would be to the left of that shown on the star map.

- What compass direction is to the left on the map?

  On February 1 at 9:00 P.M., the constellations are located to the left, or east, of the positions shown on the star map.

5

Around and Around

Locating Northern Circumpolar Constellations

What You Need to Know

Polaris is almost exactly at the north celestial pole. Polaris is called the Pole Star or North Star because it apparently remains in the same place in the sky: almost exactly above the North Pole, night after night. Polaris does move, but so slowly that you cannot see any changes in your lifetime. Because it is relatively stationary, you can use the star as a sky compass. Face Polaris and you will be facing north. Thus, to your right is east, to your left is west, and directly behind you is south. (See chapter 10, "The Dragon," for information about the movement of the North Star.)

Observe the sky for a period of time, and you will find that from night to night some stars appear to move in circular paths around Polaris. Like horses on a carousel, the stars spin around a center point, but they still stay in line with one another. Thus, the shapes of the constellations do not change even though they appear in different places during the night and on different nights of the year. The constellations are not actually moving across the sky. Their apparent motion is due to the movement of Earth as it rotates on its axis and revolves around the Sun. You can observe the movement of the stars around Polaris by sticking a pin in a star map and rotating the map on the pin.

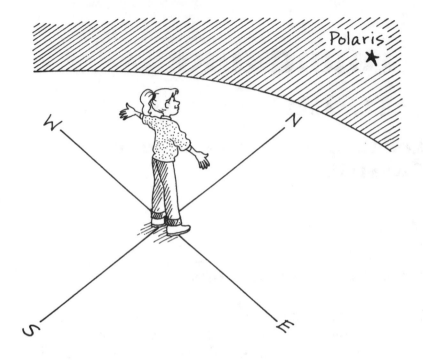

Most constellations rise and set below the horizon. The constellations near Polaris that never set are called **northern circumpolar constellations.** From latitudes 40°N or greater, the five most visible northern circumpolar constellations are Ursa Major (its asterism—the Big Dipper); Ursa Minor; **Cassiopeia** (kas-ee-oh-PEE-uh), the Queen; Cepheus; and **Draco** (DRAY-koh), the Dragon. All stars, including the stars in these constellations, are most visible at their highest point in the sky.

To determine the range of declination for northern circumpolar stars at a specific latitude, subtract the latitude of the location from 90, the latitude of the North Pole. For Philadelphia, at latitude 40°N, 90 − 40 = 50. Seen from Philadelphia, stars with a declination of +50° to +90° never set. Thus, the constellation Draco, with stars having declinations of +52° and greater, is circumpolar from Philadelphia. (For star maps that provide the declination for specific stars, see *Atlas of the Universe* by Patrick Moore [London: Rand McNally, 1994].)

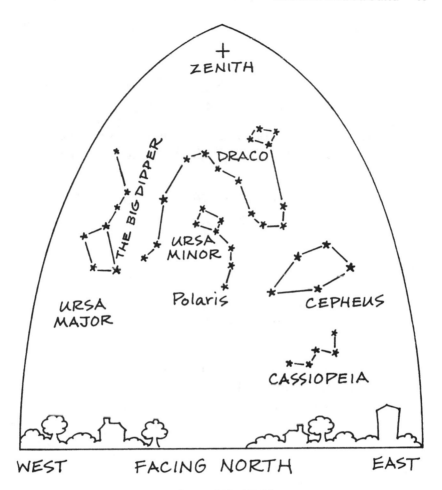

NORTHERN
CIRCUMPOLAR CONSTELLATIONS
JULY 1 at 10 P.M.
JULY 16 at 9 P.M.
AUGUST 1 at 8 P.M.

Let's Think It Through

Los Angeles is at latitude 34°N. What is the range of declination for stars in circumpolar constellations at this location?

Answers

Think!

- Los Angeles has a latitude of 34°N.

- The range of declination of circumpolar stars can be determined by subtracting the latitude of the location from 90: 90 − 34 = 56.

  The stars in circumpolar constellations seen from Los Angeles have declinations of +56° to +90°.

Exercises

1. The declinations of the stars in the constellation Cassiopeia are +56° or greater. Is this a circumpolar constellation in Dallas, Texas, at 33°N?

2. Study diagrams A and B on the next two pages and determine in which month—December or April—the constellation Cassiopeia is more visible.

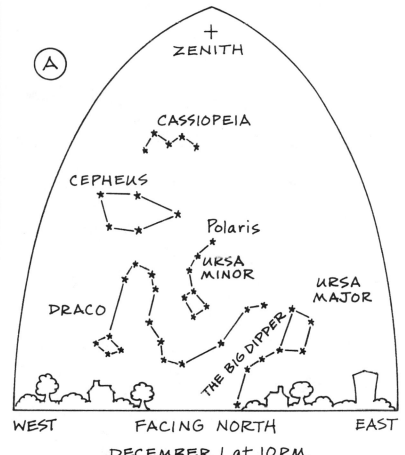

WEST   FACING NORTH   EAST

DECEMBER 1 at 10 P.M.
DECEMBER 16 at 9 P.M.
JANUARY 1 at 8 P.M.

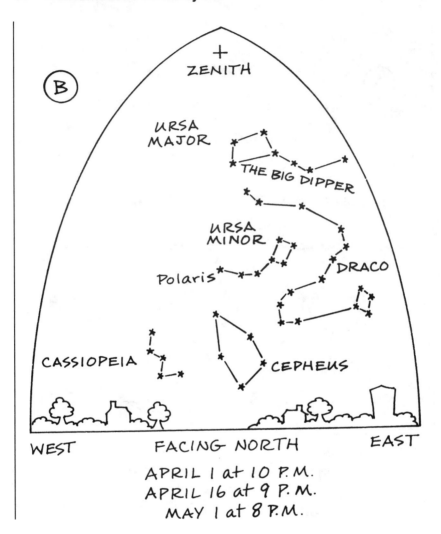

WEST   FACING NORTH   EAST

APRIL 1 at 10 P.M.
APRIL 16 at 9 P.M.
MAY 1 at 8 P.M.

Activity: STAR CLOCK

Purpose To model the apparent daily movement of circumpolar constellations.

Materials gummed stars
umbrella with 8 sections (preferably a solid, dark color)

Procedure

1. Using the gummed stars to represent the stars of the constellations Cassiopeia and Ursa Major (represented by the stars

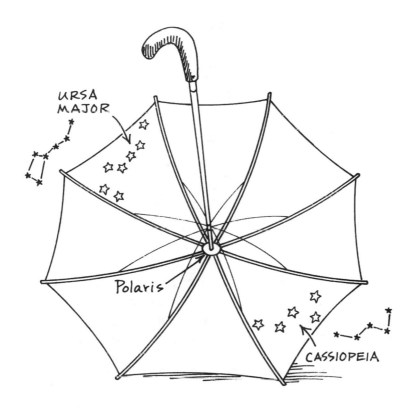

of the Big Dipper), stick the stars on the inside of the umbrella as shown in the diagram. The center of the umbrella represents Polaris.

2. Set the umbrella on a table so that the Big Dipper is at the top.

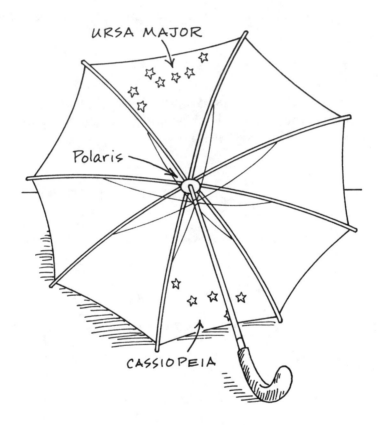

3. Rotate the umbrella one quarter turn by turning the handle slowly in a counterclockwise direction, two sections past the Big Dipper. Observe the position of the constellations in relation to one another, Polaris, and the tabletop.

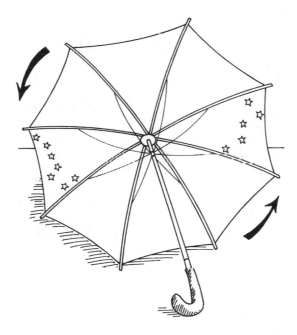

4. Repeat step 3 two more times, making observations after each quarter turn.

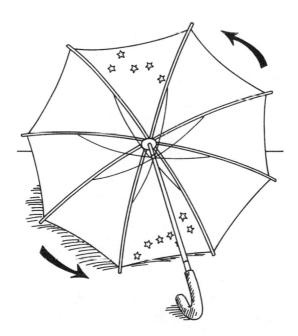

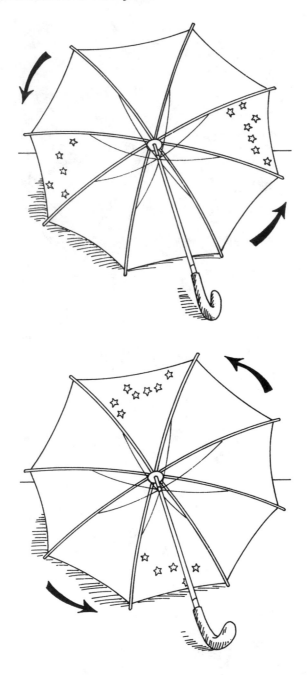

Results The center of the umbrella—Polaris—stays in the same place, and the stars of the constellations move around it.

Why?   The umbrella is a model of the northern sky. As it turns, the constellations Ursa Major and Cassiopeia move around Polaris. Northern circumpolar constellations do not actually move, but they appear to move in a circle around Polaris, similar to the way the constellations move on the umbrella, because of Earth's rotation.

The tabletop represents the northern horizon. Since the constellations stay above the horizon, they are circumpolar. Each quarter turn of the umbrella represents about 6 hours. Thus, it takes about 24 hours for the constellations to make one complete turn of 360°. A more exact time of one turn is 23 hours and 56 minutes. In a full 24 hours, the constellations would appear to rotate 361°.

Solutions to Exercises

1. *Think!*

   - Dallas has a latitude of 33°N.

   - The declination of circumpolar stars for a given location can be determined by subtracting the latitude of the location from 90: 90 − 33 = 57.

   - Stars with a declination of +57° or greater are circumpolar when viewed from Dallas.

     From Dallas, the entire constellation Cassiopeia is not circumpolar. Only the stars in Cassiopeia having declinations of +57 or greater are circumpolar as seen from Dallas.

2. *Think!*

   - The higher the star is in the sky, the more visible the star.

   - During which month of the two months shown is Cassiopeia higher in the sky?

     Cassiopeia is more visible in December than in April.

6
Great Bear

Locating the Constellation Ursa Major

What You Need to Know

The name *Ursa Major* means "Great Bear." The entire constellation of Ursa Major may not always be the easiest to find, but an asterism in it is. Ursa Major's famous asterism is made of seven bright stars forming the shape of a large dipper. Hence the name: the Big Dipper. Once you find the Big Dipper, you can then search for the rest of Ursa Major. It is easiest to find in the spring when it is high above the northern horizon.

To find the Big Dipper, look in the northern sky. Seven bright stars form what appears to be the bowl and handle of a dipper. Since Ursa Major is a northern circumpolar constellation, it circles around Polaris. Thus, the bowl of the dipper points in slightly different directions at different times during the night, and greater changes are seen from one season to the next.

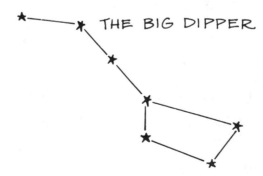

THE BIG DIPPER

As shown in the diagram, the handle of the dipper forms the bear's tail, and the bowl of the dipper forms the bear's lower back. Follow the pattern of stars along the handle down the back end of the dipper's bowl to find the stars that make up the bear's back legs. To find the faint stars making up the bear's neck and head, look past the stars at the outer end of the bowl. Below the neck are the stars that form the front legs and paws.

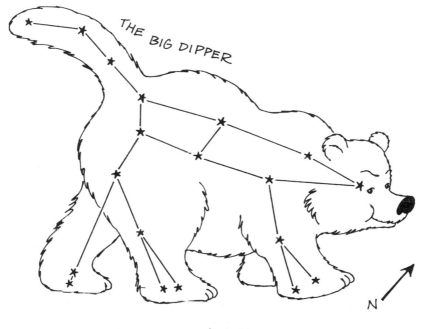

URSA MAJOR

A closer look at the second star in the handle of the Big Dipper shows that it is a **double star** (two stars that appear close together in the sky). What appears to be the larger, brighter star is called **Mizar** (MEE-zar), and the smaller, fainter star is called **Alcor** (AL-kor). Together Mizar and Alcor form what astronomers call an **optical double,** two stars that are far apart and have no relationship to each other, but appear to be very close together. These two stars appear to be close because they are both in the same line of sight for an observer on Earth. This means that when you look directly at one star, you can see the other star without moving your eyes.

The Arabs of a thousand years ago used Mizar and Alcor as a test of keen eyesight. If a person could see Alcor, his eyesight was rated as very good. Hence, these stars have been nick-named "the testers." Actually, anyone with average eyesight can see Alcor if the stars are high above the horizon and the sky is dark and clear.

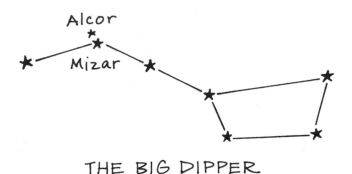

THE BIG DIPPER

Binary stars are double stars that move around a center point and are held together by their mutual gravity. A **visual binary** is a binary whose stars are far enough apart to be seen separately with the naked eye or binoculars or with a telescope. With a small telescope you could see that Mizar is also a visual binary. The separation between Mizar and its companion star is too small to see with the naked eye.

Two other stars in the Big Dipper, **Merak** (MEE-rak) and **Dubhe** (DOO-bee), are called the Pointers. If an imaginary straight line is drawn through these two stars, starting with Merak and continuing past Dubhe, the line points to Polaris. The Big Dipper is so easily found in the sky that it will be used later to help you find other, less obvious stars and constellations. It also will be used on star maps to represent Ursa Major.

Let's Think It Through

Study the diagram and choose the star group—A, B, or C—that correctly represents the location of Polaris from the Big Dipper.

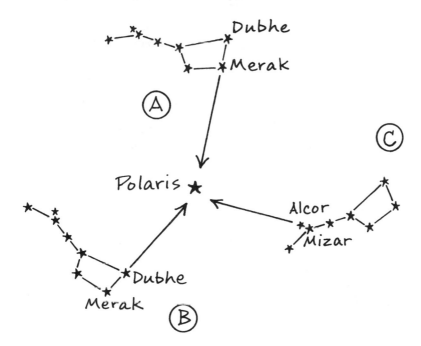

Answer

Think!

- A straight line drawn from Merak and continuing past Dubhe points to Polaris.

Position B represents the location of Polaris.

Exercise

Study the diagram and choose the position(s)—A, B, C, or D—that correctly represents the location of the Big Dipper.

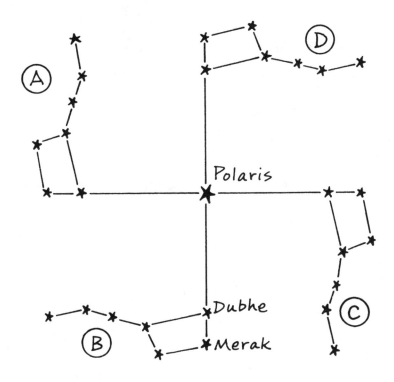

Activity: IN LINE

Purpose To prepare a model of an optical double.

Materials 2 index cards
pencil
scissors
yardstick (meterstick)

Procedure

1. Fold each card in half, placing the short sides together. Unfold the cards.

2. On one of the cards, draw a star large enough to cover half of the card.

3. Draw a dashed line around the star as shown in the diagram.

4. Place the two cards together and cut out the star in both cards by cutting along the dashed line. Make sure to cut through both layers of paper.

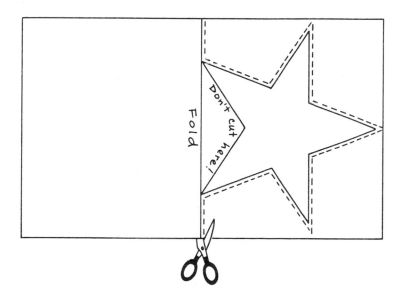

5. Separate the cards and label them by writing 1 on the star portion of one of them and 2 on the other star.

6. Bend the cards along the fold line so that the stars stand up when the uncut half of the card is placed on a flat surface.

7. Lay the measuring stick on a table so that the zero end is near the edge of the table and facing you.

8. Stand star 1 on the zero end of the measuring stick and star 2 on the opposite end of the stick.

9. Look at the stars at eye level, positioning yourself directly in front of star 1.

10. Move your head to the left until you are able to see most of star 2.

Results When viewed from a position directly in front of the stars, star 1 blocks your view of star 2. Both stars are seen when viewed from an angle, and they appear to be close together.

Why? When you are in front of the nearest star, it blocks your view of the star behind it. Looking at the stars from a slight angle allows both stars to be seen. The stars appear close to each other because they are in the same line of sight. The paper stars are models of an optical double, such as the one formed by the stars Mizar and Alcor. They appear to be close together but are not physically near each other. Viewed from Earth, Mizar and Alcor can be seen as separate stars.

Solution to Exercise

Think!

- The Big Dipper is an asterism in the circumpolar constellation Ursa Major. Thus, the asterism moves around Polaris in a circular path.

  All positions—A, B, C, and D—represent the correct location of the Big Dipper.

7
Little Bear
Locating the Constellation Ursa Minor

What You Need to Know

The name *Ursa Minor* means "Little Bear." This constellation is more commonly known as the Little Dipper. The upward bend in the dipper's handle forms the bear's tail, and the bowl is the bear's chest. It certainly takes much imagination to find the remaining parts of the bear, but the dipper is found by looking toward the north.

THE LITTLE DIPPER

URSA MINOR

Stars in the sky seem to be always moving except for the one at the end of the handle of the Little Dipper. This star is Polaris, or the North Star or Pole Star. Polaris appears to stay in one place because Earth's axis points to it.

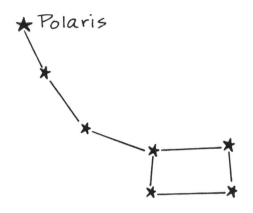

THE LITTLE DIPPER

Polaris can only be seen by observers in the Northern Hemisphere. Its location above the northern horizon depends on the latitude of the observer. If one could move quickly from the equator to the North Pole, Polaris would first be visible at the northern horizon and then appear to move above the horizon until it is directly overhead.

The angle of Polaris above the northern horizon for any observer is equal to the observer's latitude north of the equator. The observer in the diagram is at latitude 40°N. Note that the angle of Polaris above the northern horizon for the observer is 40°.

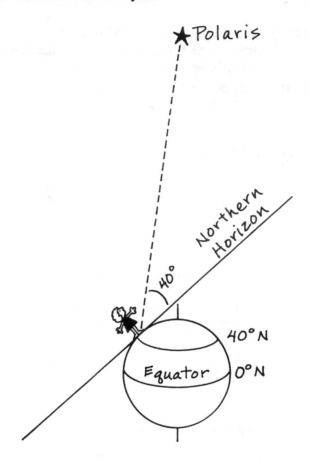

Let's Think It Through

Use the map on the next page to answer the following questions:

1. Where would observer A look for Polaris?

2. Which observer(s) would be unable to see Polaris?

Polaris
★

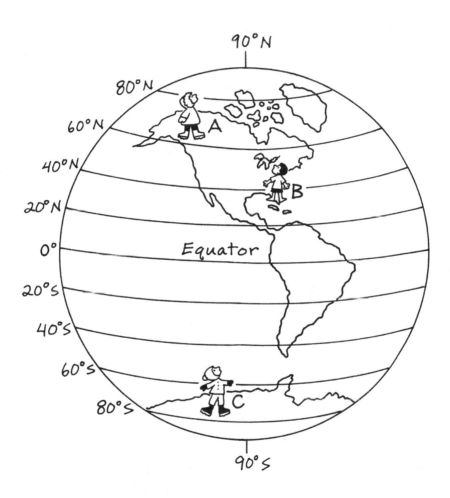

Answers

1. **Think!**

   • The angle of Polaris above the northern horizon is equal to the northern latitude of the observer.

   • Observer A is at latitude 60°N.

   Observer A would look 60° above his northern horizon to see Polaris.

2. **Think!**

   • Observers in the Southern Hemisphere cannot see Polaris.

   • Which observer is south of the equator?

   Observer C cannot see Polaris.

Exercises

1. Read the clues given about two observers, Ginger and Calvin, and determine the following:

   a. At what latitude is Ginger?

   b. Where does Calvin see Polaris?

   Clues

   • Ginger sees Polaris directly overhead.

   • Calvin is at latitude 40°N.

2. The stars in the diagram on the next page show the position of Polaris viewed from a ship at three different latitudes. At which position of Polaris is the ship closest to the equator?

Activity: ABOVE THE HORIZON

Purpose   To determine how Polaris can appear to be in
different positions.

Materials   masking tape
3 feet (0.9 m) of string
penny
ruler
yardstick (meterstick)
marking pen
index card
adult helper

Procedure

1. Tape one end of the string to the coin.

2. Ask your adult helper to tape the free end of the string to the center of the top of a doorjamb so that the coin hangs about 6 inches (15 cm) over your head when you stand in the doorway. *NOTE: Choose a doorway leading into a second room that has a far wall.*

3. Place a piece of masking tape about 1 inch (2.5 cm) long on the floor beneath the hanging coin. Mark an X on the tape.

4. Draw a thick straight line across the center of the index card. Write HORIZON beneath the line.

5. Measure 6 feet (1.8 m) from the X to a point on the floor of the first room, and place another piece of tape on the floor. Mark this tape with an E.

6. Stand behind the tape labeled E, close one eye, and look at the coin.

7. While you are looking at the coin, ask your helper to tape the card to the far wall of the second room so that the line on the card and the bottom of the coin line up.

8. As you look at the coin, slowly walk toward the X until you are standing on the tape directly beneath the coin. As you walk, notice how the bottom of the coin lines up with the card, wall, or ceiling.

Results   The coin appears to rise above the horizon line on the card as you walk toward the X.

Why?   The height of the coin above the horizon, like the angle of Polaris, depends on your location when viewing it. In this experiment the tape marked X represents the North Pole; the tape marked E, the equator; the coin, Polaris; and the line on the card, the horizon. As you move from the E toward the X, the height of the coin above the horizon line increases until, at the X, the coin is directly overhead. As in this experiment, if one could move quickly from the equator to the North Pole, the location of Polaris would seem first to be at the horizon and then appear to move above the horizon until it is directly overhead.

Solutions to Exercises

1a. *Think!*

- Ginger sees Polaris. Thus, she is in northern latitudes.

- At what angle to the horizon is Polaris when it is straight overhead? Ninety degrees.

- Since the angle of Polaris above the horizon is equal to the latitude of the observer, what is Ginger's latitude?

  Ginger is at 90°N, which is at the North Pole.

b. *Think!*

- The latitude of the observer is equal to the angle of Polaris above the northern horizon.

  Calvin sees Polaris at a 40° angle above the northern horizon.

2. *Think!*

- The closer Polaris is to the horizon, the closer the observer is to the equator.

- In which position is Polaris closest to the horizon?

  The ship is closest to the equator when Polaris is in position C.

8

The Queen

Locating the Constellation Cassiopeia

What You Need to Know

At latitudes of 40°N or greater, Cassiopeia, the Queen, is a northern circumpolar constellation. It is very noticeable in the northern sky and is easiest to see in the autumn, when it is at its highest point above the northern horizon. It is an M- or W-shaped group of stars, depending on its position in the sky. It is located on the opposite side of Polaris from the Big Dipper and about the same distance away. The W shape opens toward Polaris. The Big Dipper can be used to locate Cassiopeia. From the Big Dipper's Pointer stars (Merak and Dubhe), find Polaris and follow an imaginary line beyond Polaris to a point near the star **Caph** (KAF) at one end of Cassiopeia.

The constellation appears to be dimmer and much larger in the spring, when it is near the horizon, than at the same time of night in the autumn, when it is high in the sky. Whenever Cassiopeia, other constellations, the Sun, or the Moon are near the horizon, they appear larger than when they are higher in the sky.

The Greeks imagined that the stars in Cassiopeia form a queen sitting on her throne. Queen Cassiopeia boasted about how beautiful she and her daughter, **Andromeda** (an-DRAH-muh-duh), were. In the autumn, Cassiopeia is high in the northern sky, and the star Caph in the constellation, on the queen's right shoulder,

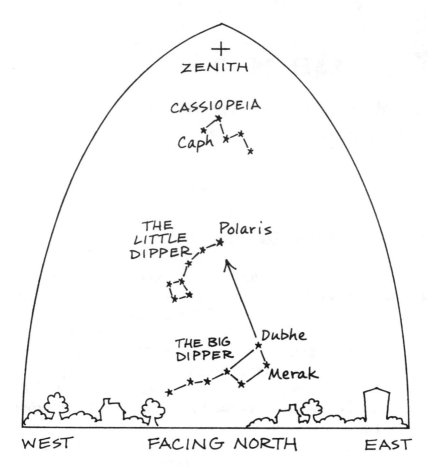

ZENITH

CASSIOPEIA

Caph

THE LITTLE DIPPER   Polaris

THE BIG DIPPER   Dubhe

Merak

WEST   FACING NORTH   EAST

NOVEMBER 1 at 10 P.M.
NOVEMBER 16 at 9 P.M.
DECEMBER 1 at 8 P.M.

points west. The queen is imagined as sitting on her throne, gazing at herself in a mirror, but she slowly turns in a counterclockwise direction from day to day until, in the spring, she is upside down and closer to the northern horizon. Her upside-down position was said to be punishment for her bragging. But, as time passes, she returns to her upright position.

CASSIOPEIA, THE QUEEN

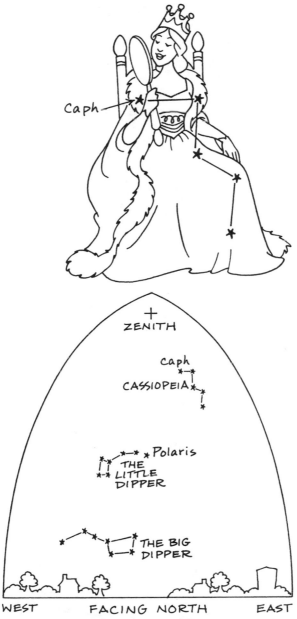

Caph

ZENITH

Caph

CASSIOPEIA

Polaris
THE
LITTLE
DIPPER

THE BIG
DIPPER

WEST   FACING NORTH   EAST

OCTOBER 1 at 10 P.M.
OCTOBER 16 at 9 P.M.
NOVEMBER 1 at 8 P.M.

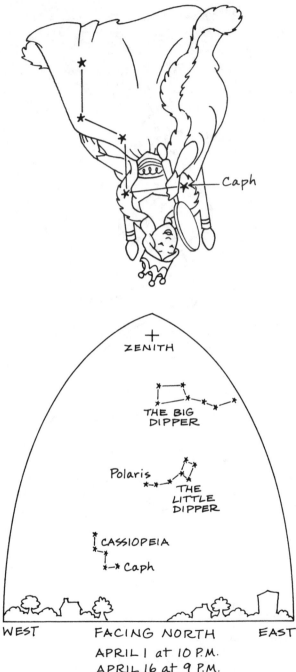

Caph

ZENITH

THE BIG
DIPPER

Polaris
THE
LITTLE
DIPPER

CASSIOPEIA

Caph

WEST   FACING NORTH   EAST
APRIL 1 at 10 P.M.
APRIL 16 at 9 P.M.
MAY 1 at 8 P.M.

This constellation is of special interest because in 1572, Tycho Brahe (TEE-koh BRAH, 1546–1601), a Danish astronomer, observed what appeared to be a new star in the constellation Cassiopeia. It was located near the queen's right hip. At its brightest, this star could be seen during the daytime. Within 2 years, the star disappeared from view. This star, and others that suddenly appear as bright new stars, are not new. They are stars too faint to see that suddenly explode, resulting in a great increase in brightness, and after a time fade out of sight again. They are a type of **variable star** (a single star that changes in brightness over time) called **novae,** from the Latin *stella nova,* meaning "new star." The nova in Cassiopeia was named Tycho's star in his honor. Generally, a nova explosion affects only the star's outer layer. The star exists both before and after the explosion. There are stars in which nova explosions have occurred more than once.

There are three types of variable stars: **eruptive variables** (stars that change in brightness because they experience explosions) such as a nova, **eclipsing variables** (stars that are concealed by another star that is in the observer's line of vision and blocks the light of the star behind it for a period of time), and **pulsating variables** (stars that periodically brighten and fade as their outer layers contract and expand). **Chi** (KYE), the center star in Cassiopeia's W, is a pulsating variable. Since its brightness changes in an unpredictable time period, it is called an **irregular pulsating variable.**

Let's Think It Through

1. Study the diagram and determine at which point—A, B, C, or D—Cassiopeia would be located.

A   C

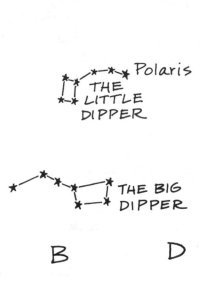

Polaris

THE
LITTLE
DIPPER

THE BIG
DIPPER

B   D

2. Study the diagrams and determine which one—A, B, or C—represents the changes of a variable star.

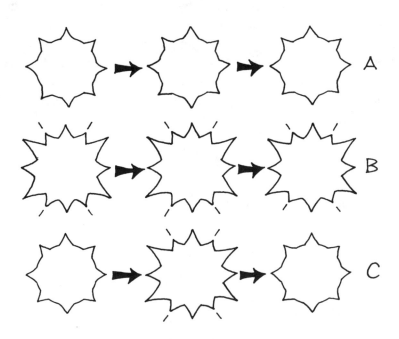

A

B

C

Answers

1. ***Think!***

   - Cassiopeia is on the opposite side of Polaris from the Big Dipper and about the same distance away.

   - An imaginary line from the Big Dipper's Pointers (Merak and Dubhe) beyond Polaris passes near Cassiopeia.

   Cassiopeia is at location C.

2. ***Think!***

   - A variable star changes in brightness over time.

   - Which diagram shows a star that is changing in brightness?

   Diagram C represents a variable star.

Exercises

1. The sky map on the next page shows the position of Cassiopeia if you face north around 10:00 P.M. during four different seasons. Study the map and determine which position—A, B, C, or D—shows Cassiopeia during the autumn in her upright position.

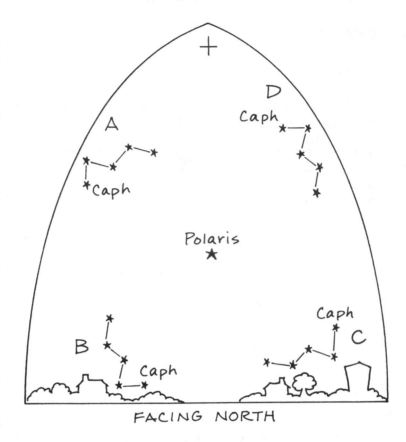

FACING NORTH

2. The diagram shows the same section of the nighttime sky on the same date in three different years. What type of star is represented?

August 6, 1959   August 6, 1960   August 6, 1961

Activity: SHRINKING

Purpose   To determine why constellations appear to decrease in size as they rise above the horizon.

Materials   drawing compass
index card
sharpened pencil
clock or watch
adult helper

Procedure

1. Ask an adult to use the point of the compass to make a small hole in the center of the index card.

2. Just after dark on a clear night in the spring, stand outdoors and find Cassiopeia in the northern sky.

Note: During another season, choose another constellation near the horizon for the activity. Repeat the activity in the spring, when Cassiopeia can be seen.

3. Close one eye and use your open eye to look through the hole in the card and again find Cassiopeia. Notice how much of the hole is filled by the constellation.

Note: If you cannot see all of the constellation through the opening, the hole is too small. Use the pencil to make the hole larger. If the constellation fills only a small part of the opening, the hole is too large. Repeat step 1, making a smaller hole.

4. Look at the constellation again without the card, then again through the hole in the card. Compare the appearance of sizes of the constellation with and without the card.

5. Repeat steps 2 and 3 every hour for at least 3 or more hours. Make note of how the constellation fits into the hole at different times of the night.

   Note: It will be worth staying up late to observe the brightness of the stars. Because the sky is darker the farther the sun is below the horizon, the stars appear brighter.

Results   Without the card, the constellation appears largest when it is nearest the horizon. It fits into the hole in the card the same way regardless of its position in the sky.

Why?   Since the constellation fits inside the hole in the card the same way whether it is at the horizon or higher in the sky, the constellation does not shrink as it rises. The apparent shrinking of the constellation as it rises is an **optical illusion** (a false mental image). First, the constellation is not rising; Earth is revolving on its axis. This causes the position of the constellation to change. Any actual difference in the constellation's distance from you at the horizon or higher in the sky is not significant.

Things on Earth at the horizon, such as buildings and trees, are very close to you. Experience has taught you that things appear larger when close than when far away. Thus, when the constellation is near the horizon, your brain interprets it as being closer and larger than when it is above you and surrounded by the expanse of the heavens. Even though you now know the truth, the constellation will still appear larger at the horizon.

Solutions to Exercises

1. *Think!*

    • When Caph points west, the queen is upright.

    • Which location—A, B, C, or D—shows Caph pointing west?

    • Facing north, west is to the left.

    Position D shows Cassiopeia upright in autumn.

2. *Think!*

    • What type of star is too faint to see, then suddenly becomes very bright and after a while fades out of sight again?

    The star is a nova.

9
The King

Locating the Constellation Cepheus

What You Need to Know

Accompanying Cassiopeia in the sky is her husband, Cepheus, the King. The stars of this constellation are much more difficult to find than the W shape of the queen's stars. The most obvious of Cepheus's stars are five that, when visually connected, form what looks like a simple drawing of a house. As with his queen, it takes a vivid imagination to picture the king sitting on his throne.

At latitudes of 40°N or greater, Cepheus is a northern circumpolar constellation near the star Polaris. To find Cepheus, face north and mentally draw a line from the star Caph in Cassiopeia to Polaris. The W shape of Cassiopeia points toward Cepheus. The star at the king's right knee (the peak of the house's roof), **Er Rai** (ehr RYE), will be close to this line and about two-thirds of the way from Caph to Polaris.

The main interest in Cepheus is one of its stars, **Delta Cephei** (DEL-tuh SEE-fee-eye). Delta Cephei is a type of pulsating variable star. *Pulsating* describes its rhythmic contractions and expansions as the star not only increases and decreases in size but also changes in brightness and apparent color. Delta Cephei and other pulsating variable stars that change in size, brightness, and color in a predictable time period are called **Cepheids** (SEH-fee-ids), after Delta Cephei. The predictable period of time in which Delta Cephei changes is about 5.4 days. During this time

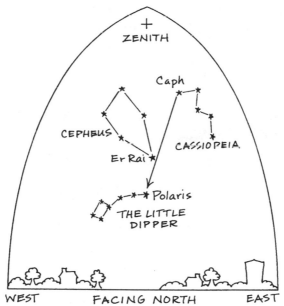

ZENITH

Caph

CEPHEUS

CASSIOPEIA.

Er Rai

Polaris

THE LITTLE
DIPPER

WEST   FACING NORTH   EAST

OCTOBER 1 at 10 P.M.
OCTOBER 16 at 9 P.M.
NOVEMBER 1 at 8 P.M.

Er Rai

CEPHEUS,
THE KING

its color changes from yellow to orange and back to yellow again. Generally, Cepheids have periods from about 1 to 50 days.

Let's Think It Through

1. Study the graph for an imaginary star called Cepheid A and answer the following:

a. What is the star's period of change in brightness?

b. On what date is the star the least bright?

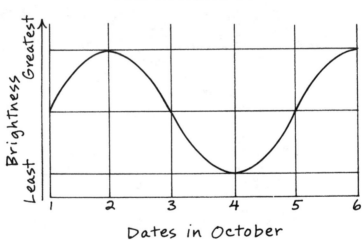

CHANGE IN BRIGHTNESS
FOR CEPHEID A

Brightness   Greatest ... Least

Dates in October

2. Which star—A, B, C, D, or E—in Cepheus is closest to Polaris?

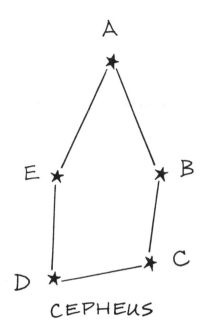

CEPHEUS

Answer

1a. *Think!*

- How many days does it take for Cepheid A to make a complete cycle in its brightness change? To determine this, imagine a dot on the graph on day 1 (October 1), where the pattern starts, and a second dot on the date where the pattern starts to repeat itself (October 5).

- The number of days between the imaginary dots equals the period of brightness variation for the Cepheid.

- How many days are there between October 1 and 5? Subtract the dates: 5 – 1 = ? Or count the days, starting with October 2 as day 1 and stopping at October 5.

The period of change in brightness for Cepheid A is 4 days.

b. Think!

- What part of the graph indicates the least brightness? The bottom.

- On which date is the pattern closest to the bottom of the graph?

The star is least bright on October 4.

2. Think!

- The star at the king's knee (the peak of the house's roof) is closest to Polaris.

Star A is closest to Polaris.

Exercises

1. Study the diagram and determine which position—A, B, or C—is the correct location for Cepheus.

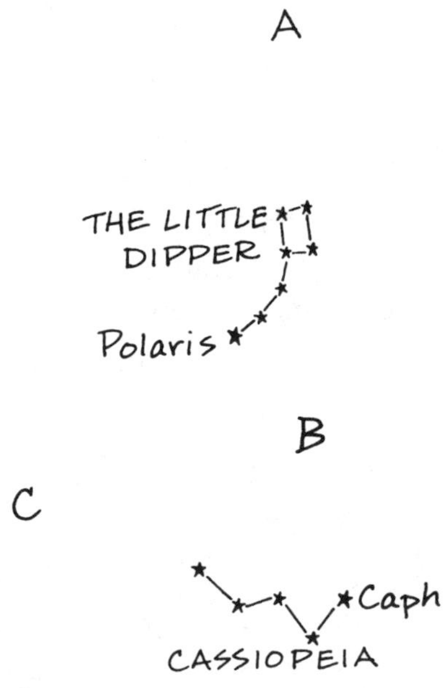

A

THE LITTLE
DIPPER

Polaris

B

C

Caph

CASSIOPEIA

2. Study the graph for an imaginary star called Cepheid B and answer the following:

a. What is the star's period of change in brightness?

b. On what date is the star the brightest?

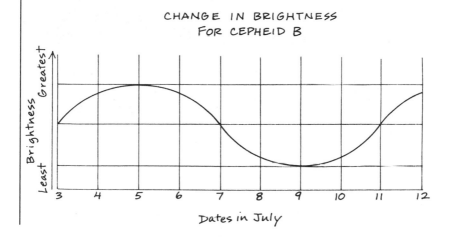

CHANGE IN BRIGHTNESS
FOR CEPHEID B

Dates in July

Activity: CHANGING

Purpose To model a Cepheid's change in size.

Materials 9-inch (22.5-cm) round balloon
watch or clock with a second hand

Procedure

1. Slightly inflate the balloon.

2. Holding the neck of the balloon, twist the balloon a half turn to keep the air inside the balloon. This size of the balloon represents star size A.

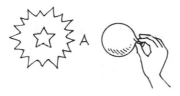

3. With the end of the balloon in your mouth, slightly untwist the neck and very slowly inflate the balloon some more for 5 seconds. Again, seal off the neck by twisting it closed. This represents size B.

4. Holding the neck of the balloon in one hand and the inflated balloon in the other, slightly untwist the balloon and very slowly allow enough air to escape so that the balloon is again as large as size A.

Results   The balloon increases and decreases in size.

Why?   The balloon changes in size as the **air pressure** (the force air puts on things) inside the balloon changes. Cepheids are pulsating variable stars whose outer layers expand and contract. Like the balloon, Cepheids change size depending on internal pressures. These stars are not at **equilibrium** (a state of balance in opposing forces). Their gravity pulling inward does not equal the pressure pushing outward. When gravity is the greater force, the star contracts. When internal pressure is the greater force, the star expands. As Cepheids change size, they also change in temperature and give off varying amounts of light.

When a Cepheid **contracts** (moves closer together), it gets smaller and hotter. With an increase in temperature, the star gives off more light energy, and thus it is brighter. As the star **expands** (spreads out), it gets larger and cooler, gives off less light energy, and is less bright. Changes in temperature result in color changes. Cepheids generally change from pale yellow at their highest temperature to yellow or orange at their coolest temperature.

Solutions to Exercises

1. *Think!*

- The star at the peak of the roof of Cepheus is located near an imaginary line connecting Polaris and Caph, in Cassiopeia.

- The W shape of Casseopeia points toward Cepheus.

  Position B is the location for Cepheus.

2a. *Think!*

- How many days does it take for the change in brightness to make a complete cycle? Imagine a dot on the graph on July 3, where the pattern starts, and a second dot on July 11, where the pattern starts to repeat itself.

- How many days are there between July 3 and 11? Subtract the dates: $11 - 3 = ?$

  The period of change in brightness for Cepheid B is 8 days.

b. *Think!*

- What part of the graph indicates the greatest brightness? The top.

- On which date is the pattern closest to the top of the graph?

The star is brightest on July 5.

10
The Dragon

Locating the Constellation Draco

What You Need to Know

Draco, the Dragon, is a large constellation. Unlike most constellations, its shape is easy to imagine by mentally connecting its stars. Although it contains no really bright stars, it is not difficult to find. Draco is best seen in the summer.

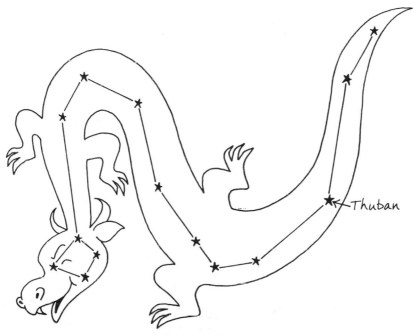

DRACO, THE DRAGON

At latitudes of 40°N or greater, Draco is a circumpolar constellation. Find Draco by looking north. The starry dragon's tail begins between the Big Dipper and the Little Dipper. The tip of the tail lies near Dubhe, a star in the bowl of the Big Dipper. The tail winds around the bowl of the Little Dipper, and the middle of the body bends toward Cepheus. The four stars that form the dragon's head point away from Cepheus and are in line with the end of the handle of the Big Dipper.

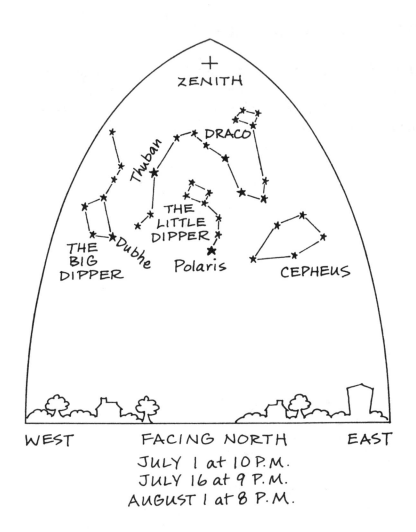

WEST   FACING NORTH   EAST
JULY 1 at 10 P.M.
JULY 16 at 9 P.M.
AUGUST 1 at 8 P.M.

The end of Earth's axis at the North Pole points to the celestial pole. The star nearest the north celestial pole is the North Star. Today the North Star is Polaris. But 5,000 years ago the axis pointed toward **Thuban** (THOO-ban), a star in the tail of Draco. The change in direction of Earth's axis is called **precession.** This change is due to the wobble of the planet as it rotates on its axis. The distance around Earth's equator is slightly larger than the distance around from pole to pole. The pull of the gravity of the Sun and Moon on Earth's bulging equator causes the planet to wobble when it spins. As a result of the wobble, the axis at the North Pole traces an imaginary circular pattern in the sky. It takes Earth's axis about 26,000 years to complete one wobble. As Earth precesses, the North Star changes. About 12,000 years from now, the bright star **Vega** (VEE-guh), in the constellation **Lyra** (LYE-ruh), the Lyre, will be the North Star.

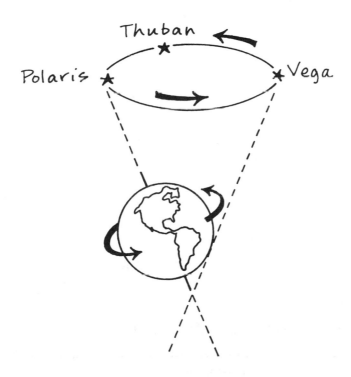

Let's Think It Through

1. Study the diagram and determine which position—A, B, C, or D—is the location of the head of Draco.

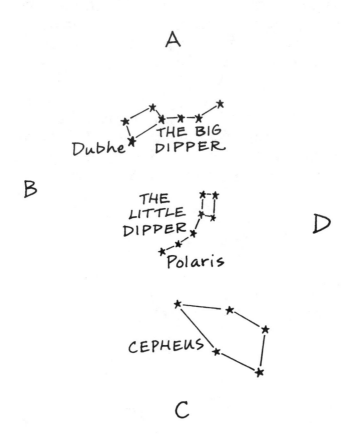

2. The diagram indicates the path of the precession of Earth's axis. Use the diagram to answer the following questions, rounding off to thousands:

   a. In what year will Thuban again be the North Star?

   b. In what year after Vega is the North Star will Polaris again be the North Star?

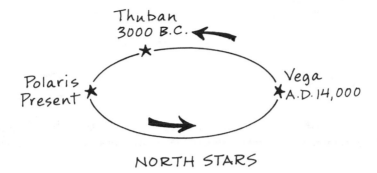

NORTH STARS

Answers

1. *Think!*

- The dragon's tail starts near Dubhe and curls around the bowl of the Little Dipper. The body points toward Cepheus, then turns back so that its head points away from Cepheus and is in line with the end of the handle of the Big Dipper.

Position D represents the location of Draco's head.

2a. *Think!*

- When was Thuban the North Star? 3000 B.C.

- How many years after 3000 B.C. will Thuban again be the North Star? Twenty-six thousand.

- Making the B.C. date a negative number, 26,000 + (− 3000) = ?

- Subtract the dates: 26,000 − 3,000 = ?

Thuban will be the North Star again in A.D. 23,000.

b. *Think!*

- It takes 26,000 years for Earth's axis to make one precession.

- Using A.D. 2000 as the present date, $26{,}000 + 2{,}000 = ?$

Polaris will be the North Star again around A.D. 28,000.

Exercise

1. Study diagrams A, B, and C. Determine which diagram shows the location of the star forming the tip of Draco's tail.

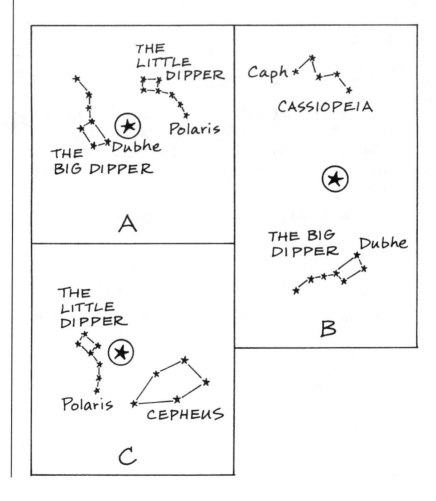

2. The circle in the diagram represents the path of Earth's precession. The dots on the circle represent the changing positions of the North Star. Study the diagram and answer these questions:

  a. In 5,000 years, the North Star will be in what constellation?

  b. After the date shown for Vega, in the constellation Lyra, in what year will Vega again become the North Star?

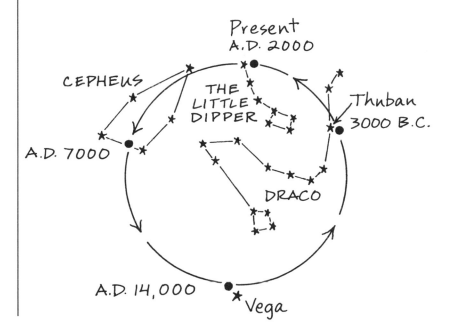

Present
A.D. 2000

CEPHEUS

THE LITTLE DIPPER

Thuban
3000 B.C.

A.D. 7000

DRACO

A.D. 14,000

Vega

Activity: WOBBLER

Purpose To demonstrate Earth's precession.

Materials drawing compass
index card
scissors
round toothpick
adult helper

Procedure

1. Use the compass to draw a 2-inch (5-cm) circle on the index card.

2. Cut out the paper circle.

3. Ask an adult to push the toothpick through the center of the circle so that about ¼ inch (0.63 cm) of the toothpick sticks out one side.

   Note: Your adult helper may need to use the point of the compass to make a starting hole in the paper for the tooth-pick to go through.

4. Place the tip of the toothpick on a flat surface, such as a table, so that the long end of the toothpick is sticking up.

5. Quickly twirl the long end of the toothpick between your fingers, then let it go.

6. Observe the movement of the top of the toothpick.

Results   As the paper circle spins, the top of the toothpick moves in a circular path.

Why?   As the circle spins, there is a shifting of the weight be-cause its shape is not perfectly round and the toothpick may not be exactly through the center of the paper. Earth, like the circle, wobbles as it rotates because it is not perfectly round. It has a slight bulge at the equator, making it larger around the equator than around from pole to pole. Earth's axis moves in a circular path as the planet wobbles. This movement is called precession. The top of the toothpick makes many revolutions as the circle spins, but it takes about 26,000 years for Earth to wobble enough for its axis to make one complete turn.

Solutions to Exercises

1. *Think!*

- The tip of Draco's tail is between the Little Dipper and the Big Dipper near Dubhe of the Big Dipper.

  Diagram A shows the star forming the tip of Draco's tail.

2a. *Think!*

- In 5,000 years, what year will it be? 2,000 + 5,000 = 7,000.

- The diagram shows the path of Earth's precession moving toward which constellation in the year A.D. 7000?

  In 5,000 years, the North Star will be in the constellation Cepheus.

b. *Think!*

- It takes the earth 26,000 years to make one precession.

- The date that Vega will again be the North Star after the date shown is calculated as 14,000 + 26,000 = ?

  After the date shown, Vega will be the North Star again in A.D. 40,000.

11
Sun Path

Locating the Zodiac Constellations

What You Need to Know

The earth and the other planets of our solar system revolve around the sun. But from Earth, it appears that the Sun and the planets move among the stars across the surface of the celestial sphere. The apparent yearly path of the Sun around the celestial sphere is called the **ecliptic** and in the diagram is a dashed line. Note that half of the ecliptic is above the celestial equator and the other half is below. (See chapter 12 for information about the high and low positions of the ecliptic.)

The ecliptic runs through a band on which 12 constellations are shown. This band is called the **zodiac,** and the constellations along the band are **zodiac constellations.** These constellations, in order as they appear, are listed in the chart on the next page.

As seen from Earth, the zodiac constellations provide a background for the other planets. This is because their orbits around the Sun all lie nearly in the same plane as Earth's orbit. The planets appear to move in paths near the ecliptic through the zodiac constellations. The planets visible with the naked eye are Mercury, Venus, Mars, Jupiter, and Saturn. A telescope is needed to view the other planets—Uranus, Neptune, and Pluto.

ZODIAC CONSTELLATIONS

Name	Pronunciation	Sun's Entry Date
Pisces, the Fish	PYE-seez	Mar 15
Aries, the Ram	AIR-eez	Apr 16
Taurus, the Bull	TOR-us	May 15
Gemini, the Twins	JEH-muh-nye	Jun 16
Cancer, the Crab	KAN-sur	Jul 17
Leo, the Lion	LEE-oh	Aug 17
Virgo, the Maiden	VUR-go	Sep 17
Libra, the Scales	LEE-bruh	Oct 18
Scorpius, the Scorpion	SKOR-pee-us	Nov 17
Sagittarius, the Archer	sa-juh-TAIR-ee-us	Dec 17
Capricornus, the Sea Goat	ka-prih-KOR-nus	Jan 15
Aquarius, the Water Bearer	uh-KWAIR-ee-us	Feb 13

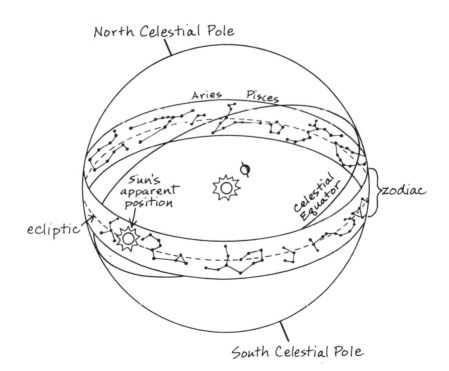

Astronomers sometimes use the zodiac constellations to point to the locations of the Sun and the planets at a particular time. At specified times, the Sun and the planets are said to be "in" constellations. The diagram below represents the position of Earth when the Sun is in Pisces. The brightness of the Sun's light prevents constellations from being seen during the day. If they could be seen, then Pisces would be visible at the end of an imaginary line from Earth through the Sun toward the constellation Pisces. March 15 through April 15 is when the Sun is in Pisces. During this time, Pisces appears behind the Sun on the ecliptic, and together they rise above the eastern horizon, move in an arched path across the southern sky, and set below the western horizon. In front and behind are the other zodiac constellations in their apparent path along the ecliptic. On either side of the zodiac are other stars and constellations, also apparently moving from east to west across the sky. The approximate dates on which the Sun enters each zodiac constellation are listed in the chart on the previous page.

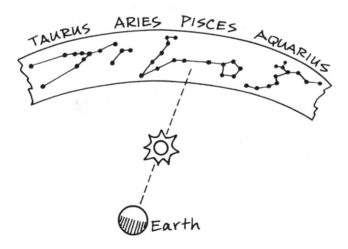

Remember, the Sun and the constellations are not actually moving across the sky. Instead, Earth is turning and you are seeing the Sun and the constellations as Earth rotates past them. Earth makes one complete rotation in about 23 hours and 56 minutes, passing by zodiac constellations plus other constellations and stars in the sky. At night, when the dark side of Earth is away from the Sun, you see constellations and stars that are on the opposite side of the ecliptic and therefore not in the daytime sky.

The Sun's apparent movement is slower than the movement of the zodiac constellations. It takes the Sun 24 hours to complete its daily journey, which is about four times longer than it takes the constellations. This time adds up, and about every 4 to 6 weeks, depending on the size of the constellation, the next zodiac constellation catches up to the Sun. After the Sun leaves Pisces, it will enter Aries, then Taurus, and so on, until it is in Pisces again.

The zodiac is also the "sun signs" of astrology. **Astrology** is a study that assumes that the positions of the zodiac constellations and other celestial bodies affect people's lives. There is no scientific evidence that this is true. Thus, astrology is considered a **pseudoscience** (a set of beliefs pretending to be scientific but not based on scientific principles). Ancient astrologers divided the zodiac into 12 parts called signs, and each sign was named after the constellation that the Sun was in at that time. For example, the sun sign of Aquarius was from January 21 through February 19, and during this period the Sun was in the constellation Aquarius. Because of precession, the established dates of the zodiac signs do not coincide with current dates when the Sun is in the zodiac constellations. Today, the astrology sign of Aquarius is still January 21 through February 19, but the Sun is in Capricornus during most of this time. Nevertheless, astrologers continue to use the ancient dates for their sun signs.

Let's Think It Through

1. Study the diagram to determine which zodiac constellation the Sun is in.

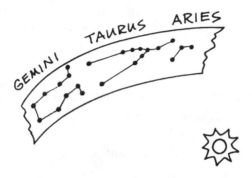

Earth

2. The diagram shows Gemini just after sunset. Which figure—A or B—shows the position of Gemini just after sunset a week or so later?

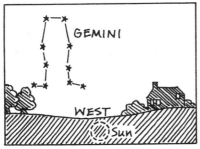

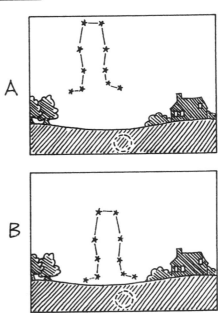

Answers

1. *Think!*

- Which constellation is in the path of a line drawn from Earth through the Sun to the zodiac?

  The Sun is in Gemini.

2. *Think!*

- The Sun and the zodiac constellations appear to rise above the eastern horizon and set below the western horizon.

- The Sun's apparent movement is slower than that of the zodiac constellations. Thus, Gemini catches up to and even passes the Sun.

Figure B shows Gemini catching up to the Sun.

Exercises

Study the diagram to answer the following:

1. When Earth is in position C, which zodiac constellation is the Sun in?

2. When Earth is in position C, which zodiac constellation can be seen in the night sky?

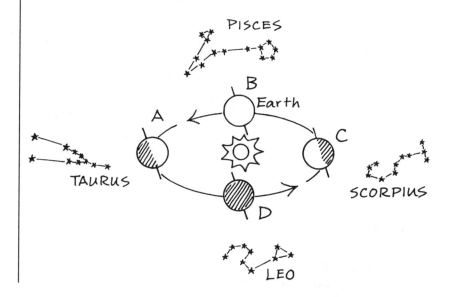

Activity: CHANGING BACKGROUND

Purpose   Determining why the apparent position of the sun
in the zodiac changes.

Materials   marking pen
12 sheets of typing paper
masking tape
helper

Procedure

1.   Print the names of the zodiac constellations on the sheets of
paper, one name per sheet.

2.   Tape 3 of the papers to each of the four walls in a room at a
height slightly higher than the height of your helper. The papers must be positioned in the order shown in the diagram.

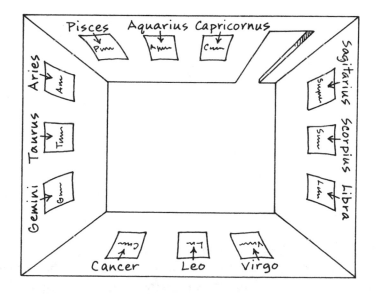

3.   Ask your helper to stand in the center of the room.

4.   Stand facing your helper so that Aries is behind your helper.

5. Walk slowly around your helper in a counterclockwise direction, but continue to face your helper.

6. Observe the constellations on the wall directly behind your helper's head as you walk. Stop when you get back to Aries.

Results Different constellations appear above your helper's head as you move.

Why? The Sun does not actually move across the sky. Instead, Earth revolves around the Sun. The stars in the constellations do not actually move across the sky. They just seem to change positions, depending on where Earth is. Your helper's head represents the Sun, and you, Earth. As Earth revolves around the Sun, different zodiac constellations are behind the

Sun. When the Sun is in a given zodiac constellation, the constellation cannot be seen because of the Sun's light. *CAUTION: Do not look at the sun. Its light can damage your eyes.*

The papers with the constellations' names represent the order of the zodiac constellations in the sky, but not their distances from one other. It takes Earth one year to make one complete trip around the Sun. During the year, the Sun appears to move into each of the 12 zodiac constellations.

Solutions to Exercises

1. *Think!*

   - What zodiac constellation is in the path of an imaginary line drawn from Earth (in position C) through the Sun?

     When Earth is in position C, the Sun is in Taurus.

2. *Think!*

   - The side of Earth away from the Sun is dark. This dark side points toward the nighttime sky.

   - Which zodiac constellation is on Earth's dark side when Earth is in position C?

     When Earth is in position C, Scorpius can be seen at night.

12
The Scales
Locating the Constellation Libra

What You Need to Know

Libra, the Scales, is the only zodiac constellation that does not represent a living thing. It represents a scale, an instrument of balance. It is the least obvious zodiac constellation because its stars are not exceptionally bright and it appears near the southern horizon. Stars near any horizon are less visible. Libra is most visible in June. (For information about the constellations around Libra, see chapter 16, "Springtime Patterns.")

Ancient stargazers thought the Sun moved around Earth. They observed that the Sun's path arches across the sky each day. At midday (noon) the path is at its peak. During the year, the peak changes from high above the horizon in the summer to low during the winter. This apparent up-and-down movement of the Sun through the seasons is due to the tilt of Earth as it revolves around the Sun. The ecliptic, the apparent path of the Sun, is tilted toward the celestial equator. For 6 months of the year, the Sun appears to be north of the celestial equator and therefore high in the daytime sky of observers in the Northern Hemisphere.

On about June 21, the Sun is farthest north of the celestial equator and its path reaches its highest point in the sky. This location is called the **summer solstice.** In the diagram, a dot marks the summer solstice. This dot is where the Sun appears to be in the sky as viewed from Earth on June 21. Because the Sun and

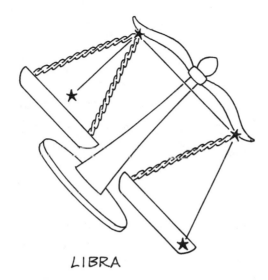

LIBRA

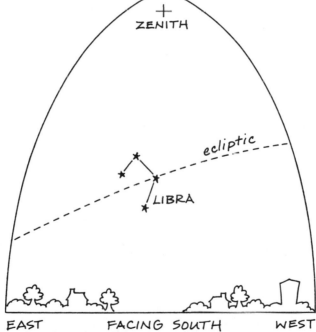

+
ZENITH

ecliptic

LIBRA

EAST   FACING SOUTH   WEST

JUNE 1 at 10 P.M.
JUNE 16 at 9 P.M.
JULY 1 at 8 P.M.

the zodiac constellations are so far from Earth, they all appear to be together on the zodiac.

For the other 6 months of the year, the Sun appears to be south of the celestial equator and low in the sky. On about December 21, the Sun is farthest south of the celestial equator and its path reaches its lowest point in the sky. This location is called the **winter solstice.**

The ecliptic crosses the celestial equator twice. The position of the Sun on about March 21 when it crosses the celestial equator and heads north is called the vernal or spring equinox. The **autumnal** or **fall equinox** is the position of the Sun on about September 23 when it crosses the celestial equator and heads south. The peak of the Sun's path at the equinoxes is about midway between the high point of summer and the low point of winter.

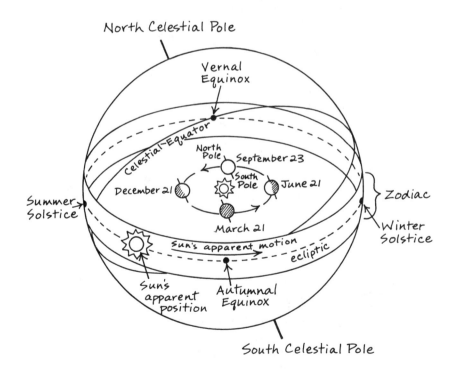

Several thousand years ago, the Sun was in Libra, the Scales, during the autumnal equinox. Because Earth wobbles ever so slightly as it spins on its axis, it precesses. After thousands of years, its axis now points in a different direction. (See chapter 10, "The Dragon," for more information about Earth's precession.) Today, because of the change in the position of Earth, the Sun is in a different zodiac constellation during the autumnal equinox. (Use the diagram in "Let's Think It Through" to discover the name of this constellation.)

Let's Think It Through

The diagram shows the approximate positions of Earth, the Sun, and the zodiac. Study the diagram and answer the following:

1. Which position—A, B, C, or D—shows Earth during the autumnal equinox?

2. Which zodiac constellation is the Sun in during the autumnal equinox?

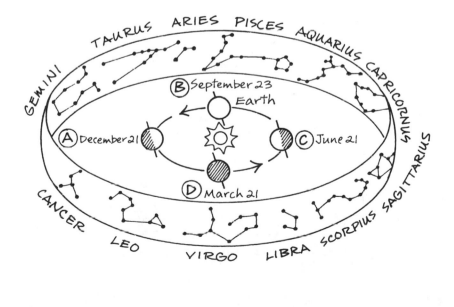

Answers

1. *Think!*

• The autumnal equinox occurs on about September 23 each year.

Position B shows Earth during the autumnal equinox.

2. *Think!*

• An imaginary line from Earth through the Sun to the zodiac shows the zodiac constellation the Sun is in.

The Sun is in Virgo during the autumnal equinox.

Exercises

The chart shows the peak of the Sun's path at noon on different days during the year. Study the chart and answer the following:

1. Which location—A, B, C, D, or E—represents the winter solstice?

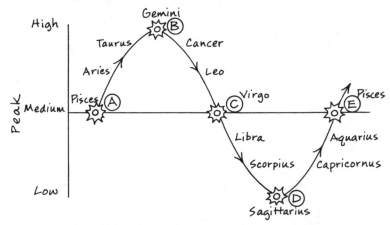

THE PEAK OF THE SUN'S PATH AT NOON

2. In which constellation is the peak highest—in Aries, Libra, or Capricornus?

Activity: HIGH AND LOW

Purpose To create a model that indicates the position of the Earth and Sun during the summer and winter solstices.

Materials scissors
ruler
1 sheet of typing paper
transparent tape
marking pen
golf-ball-size piece of modeling clay
2-inch (5-cm) -diameter circle of yellow
    construction paper
paper clip

Procedure

1. Cut two 1½-inch (3.75-cm) strips from the longest side of the typing paper.

2. Overlap and tape the ends of the strips together to form one long strip.

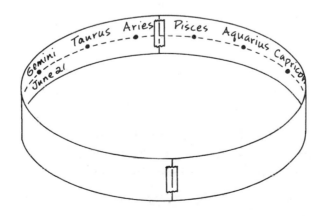

3. Draw a dashed line down the center of the strip.

4. On the dashed line, make a dot ¾ inch (2 cm) from the right end of the strip. Make 12 more dots along the line, spaced 1½ inches (3.75 cm) apart.

5. Starting at the first dot on the right end of the strip, write the following zodiac constellation names with the dates below Gemini and Sagittarius: Aries, Taurus, Gemini (June 2), Cancer, Leo, Virgo, Libra, Scorpius, Sagittarius (Dec 21), Capricornus, Aquarius, Pisces.

6. Overlap the ends of the strip so that the names are on the inside of the loop and the last, unmarked dot is covered by the dot marked Aries. Tape the ends together to make a loop. The loop represents the ecliptic.

7. Break the piece of clay in half and shape it into a marshmallow-shaped stand about 1 inch (2.5 cm) high. Set the clay stand on a table.

8. Set the paper loop on a table so that the section labeled Gemini rests on the clay stand and the section labeled Sagittarius rests on the tabletop.

9. Break off a pea-size piece of clay from the remaining piece of clay and use it to stand the yellow circle in the center of the paper loop facing Gemini. The yellow circle represents the Sun.

10. Mold the remaining clay into a ball and insert the paper clip as shown. The clay ball represents Earth, and the paper clip an observer.

11. Set the clay Earth inside the loop between the Sun and Sagittarius so that the observer faces Gemini. Observe the position of Gemini, the Sun, and the observer.

12. Move the clay Earth between the Sun and Gemini so that the observer faces Sagittarius. Observe the position of Sagittarius, the Sun, and the observer.

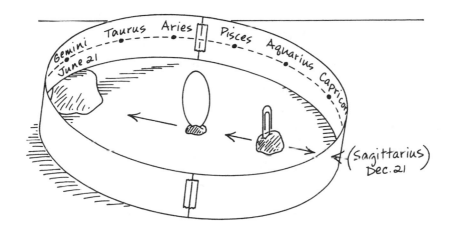

Results When the observer faces Gemini or Sagittarius, the Sun is between the observer and that constellation.

Why? June 21 is the summer solstice. On this date, the Sun is between Earth and Gemini. From Earth, the Sun appears to be on the ecliptic represented by the loop of paper. The peak of the Sun's apparent path is at its highest on June 21, when the Sun is in Gemini. This was demonstrated by placing on the clay stand the section of the loop labeled Gemini.

December 21 is the winter solstice. On this date, the Sun is between Earth and Sagittarius. Again, as viewed from Earth, the Sun appears to be on the ecliptic and is at its lowest point in the sky on December 21. This is demonstrated by placing the section of the loop labeled Sagittarius on the table.

Solutions to Exercises

1. *Think!*

   • Each day, the Sun reaches its highest point in the sky at noon.

- The winter solstice is the day when the peak of the Sun's path at noon is the lowest of the year.

- Which location shows the Sun at its lowest peak at noon?

Location D represents the winter solstice.

2. *Think!*

- Libra and Capricornus are on lines at positions representing medium to low peaks.

- Aries is on a line at a position representing a medium to high peak.

The peak of the Sun's path is highest when the Sun is in Aries than when it is in Libra or Capricornus.

13

The Teapot

Locating the Constellation Sagittarius

What You Need to Know

The constellation **Sagittarius** (sa-juh-TAIR-ee-us), the Archer, is the southernmost zodiac constellation. It rises in the southeast, moves across the southern sky near the horizon, and sets in the southwest. It is seen from early July to late September. The entire constellation was imagined by the Greeks to look like an archer, and later was thought to be a centaur—half man, half horse. It is difficult to recognize an archer or centaur, but the asterism called the Teapot is easier to find. The "steam" of the teapot is the Milky Way, which is at its brightest in Sagittarius. Preceding Sagittarius across the sky is the zodiac constellation Scorpius, the Scorpion, which has an anchorlike shape.

Sagittarius contains many **clusters** (groups of a few to many thousands of stars held together by their gravity) and nebulae. One that can be seen with the naked eye is the Lagoon Nebula, called M8. This **emission nebula** (a nebula that shines by its own light) is found above the spout of the teapot. To the naked eye, it appears as a faint cloudy patch. With binoculars, the observer sees twinkling stars surrounded by a glowing background, and with a telescope, a grand star cluster in a glowing cloud. It is called the Lagoon Nebula because dark clouds of dust cut across it that look like **lagoons** (large bodies of water).

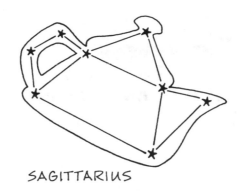

SAGITTARIUS

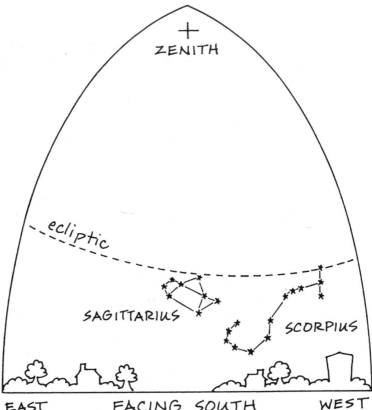

+
ZENITH

ecliptic

SAGITTARIUS

SCORPIUS

EAST   FACING SOUTH   WEST
AUGUST 1 at 10 P.M.
AUGUST 16 at 9 P.M.
SEPTEMBER 1 at 8 P.M.

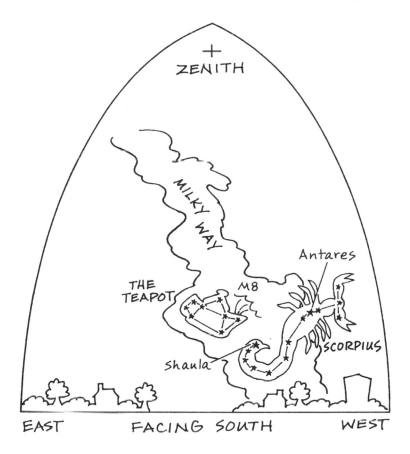

The steam from the teapot appears to be not only rising but flowing westward onto Scorpius. Following a line westward from the spout of the teapot is the bright, reddish star **Antares** (an-TAIR-eez), in Scorpius. This star represents the heart of the scorpion. Closer to the Teapot are two stars in the scorpion's tail. The brighter one is **Shaula** (SHOW-luh), which is Arabic for "the sting."

Traditionally, only 12 zodiac constellations are listed, and most diagrams and descriptions of the zodiac show only 12, but there is a thirteenth constellation through which the Sun enters each year around November 30. This often forgotten constellation is **Ophiuchus** (oh-fee-YOO-kus), the Serpent Bearer. This constellation represents a physician holding a snake. (Our early ancestors associated snakes with healing.) The snake is a separate constellation called **Serpens** (SUR-penz) and is the only divided constellation. **Serpens Caput** (KAH-put), Head of the Snake, is on the west side of Ophicuhus, and **Serpens Cauda** (KOW-duh), Tail of the Snake, is on the east side. Ophiuchus can be found by looking north of Scorpius. The small, lower part of Ophiuchus that lies on the ecliptic is between the Teapot and Scorpius.

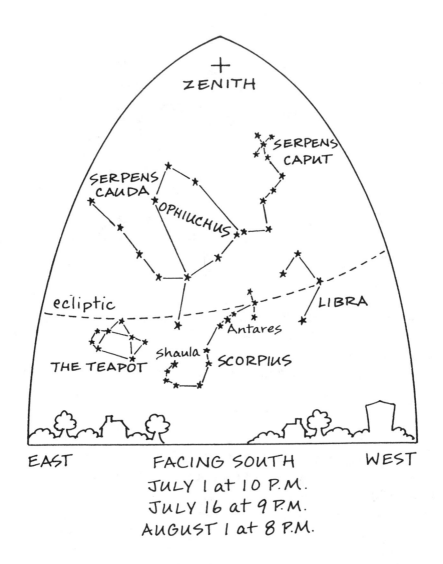

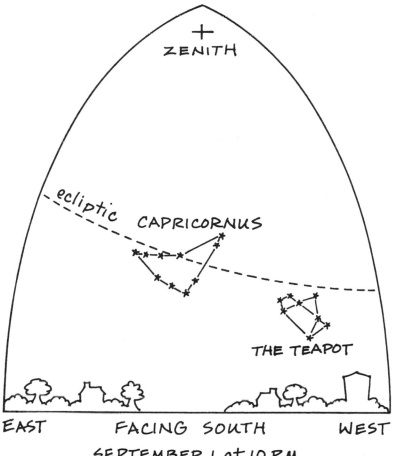

ZENITH

ecliptic

CAPRICORNUS

THE TEAPOT

EAST   FACING SOUTH   WEST

SEPTEMBER 1 at 10 P.M.
SEPTEMBER 16 at 9 P.M.
OCTOBER 1 at 8 P.M.

Another summertime zodiac constellation is Capricornus, the Sea Goat. The figure is imagined as having the head and forelegs of a goat and the tail of a fish. Actually, it looks more like an arrowhead. This constellation is dim but can be located to the east of the Teapot.

Let's Think It Through

Which statement describes the Lagoon Nebula?

a. A dark shape

b. Made of dust and gas

c. Found in the constellation Scorpius

Answer

Think!

- While parts of it are dark, most of this nebula is bright because its gases are hot enough to give off light.

- All nebulae are made of dust and gas.

- The Lagoon Nebula is near Sagittarius but is not within Scorpius.

   Statement B describes the Lagoon Nebula, because, like all nebulae, it is made of dust and gas.

Exercise

Which position—A, B, or C—on the diagram on the next page represents the location of the thirteenth zodiac constellation?

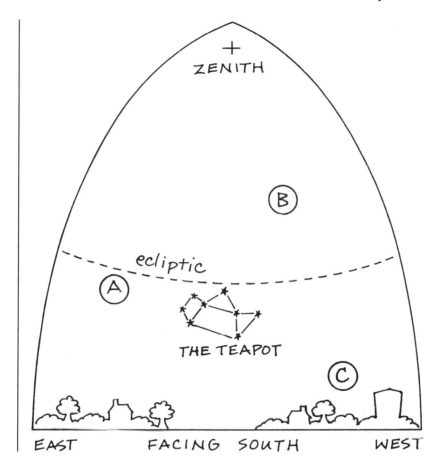

Activity: THE DARK TRAIL

Purpose   To demonstrate why the Lagoon Nebula has dark
areas.

Materials   one-hole paper punch
index card
ruler
transparent tape

Procedure

1. Punch 2 holes in the index card as shown.

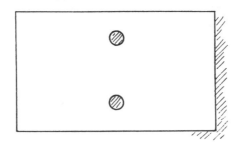

2. Tear off a piece of tape about 1 inch (2.5 cm) long and place it over one of the holes.

3. Face an open window that does not have direct sunlight.

CAUTION: Never look directly at the Sun, because doing so can damage your eyes.

4. Close one eye, and hold the card in front of your open eye. Look through each hole and observe the amount of light that you can see through the holes.

5. Tear off a second piece of tape about 1½ inches (3.75 cm) long. Stick one end of the tape next to the covered hole. Loop the tape over the hole by supporting it with the point of the pencil and attaching the other end to the opposite side of the hole as shown. Remove the pencil.

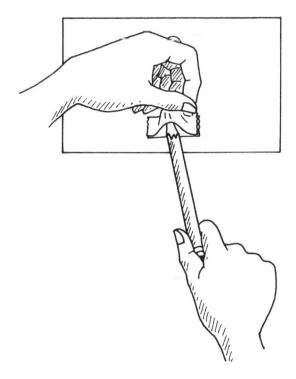

6. Again, look through the holes in the card, observing the amount of light you can see through each hole.

7. Repeat steps 5 and 6 five times, increasing the length of tape by about ½ inch (1.25 cm) each time and attaching each loop over the preceding one. The loops should not stick to each other.

Results   The amount of light coming through the uncovered hole does not change. But the light coming through the covered hole decreases as each piece of tape is added, until little or no light can be seen.

Why? The clear plastic is **transparent,** meaning that light passes straight through it. One's view changes slightly when looking through single or even double layers of transparent materials. But as the layers of transparent material separated by layers of air increase, more and more light is blocked. The same thing is true when looking through a nebula made of clouds of dust and gas. The dark areas in the Lagoon Nebula are due to interstellar materials that block light.

Solutions to Exercise

Think!

- The thirteenth zodiac constellation is Ophiuchus.
- A small, lower portion of Ophiuchus is on the ecliptic between the Teapot and Scorpius.
- Most of Ophiuchus is above Scorpius.
- Scorpius is located to the west of the Teapot.

  Position B represents the location of Ophiuchus.

14
The Lion
Locating the Constellation Leo

What You Need to Know

Leo, the Lion, is a zodiac constellation found high in the southern sky near the zenith from early April to late June. Two stars, **Megrez** (MEH-grez) and **Phecda** (FEK-duh), in the bowl of the Big Dipper, can be used to point the way to Leo. Using the star map, face north and extend an imaginary line southward from these two stars to a bright star. This star is **Regulus** (REH-gyuh-lus) which is at the heart of the lion.

Once you have found Regulus, face south and locate the remaining stars in the lion. Facing south, the lion will appear right side up. To the west lie five stars that, with Regulus, are in the shape of a backward question mark. These form the lion's head. The body and tail of the lion lie east of Regulus.

Stars are not all the same distance from Earth. The star Regulus is about 502 trillion miles (802 trillion km) from Earth, and **Denebola** (duh-NEB-uh-luh), the star in Leo's tail, is about 230 trillion miles (368 trillion km) away. Since the distance of stars is so very great, astronomers use a measuring unit called the **light-year (ly)**. One ly is the distance that light travels in 1 year, or about 5.9 trillion miles (9.4 trillion km). It takes about 85 years for the light from Regulus to reach Earth. This is a distance of 85 ly. Light from the star Denebola takes about 39 years to reach Earth. Thus, its distance is 39 ly from Earth.

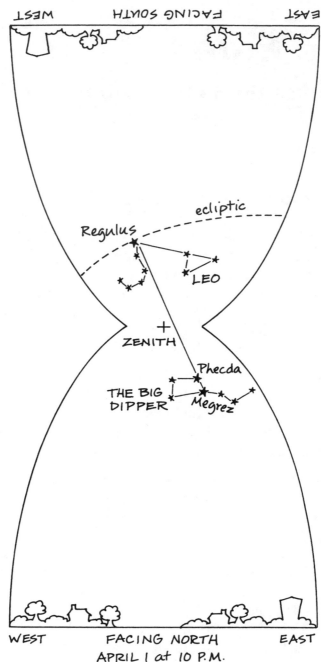

WEST   FACING SOUTH   EAST

ecliptic

Regulus

LEO

+
ZENITH

Phecda

THE BIG
DIPPER   Megrez

WEST   FACING NORTH   EAST
APRIL 1 at 10 P.M.
APRIL 16 at 9 P.M.
MAY 1 at 8 P.M.

LEO THE LION

One method that astronomers use to find the distance of nearby stars is to measure their **parallax** (the apparent shift in position of an object when viewed from different places). To understand this method of measuring, place your thumb near your nose, then look at it, closing one eye at a time. Your thumb seems to jump from side to side as you see a different background behind it. Stars, like your thumb, seem to move when viewed from different positions. The greater the distance between the two viewing places, the greater the jump, or parallax, of the star.·

Stellar parallax is the parallax of a star. To measure the stellar parallax, astronomers photograph the sky on one night, then photograph it again 6 months later when Earth is on the opposite side of its **orbit** (the path of one celestial body around another) around the Sun. This provides viewing spots separated by a distance equal to the diameter of Earth's orbit around the Sun, which is about 187 million miles (300 million km). A comparison of the two photographs shows how much a star shifts. The closer the star is to Earth, the greater its stellar parallax. The diagram greatly exaggerates the stellar parallax of even the closest star.

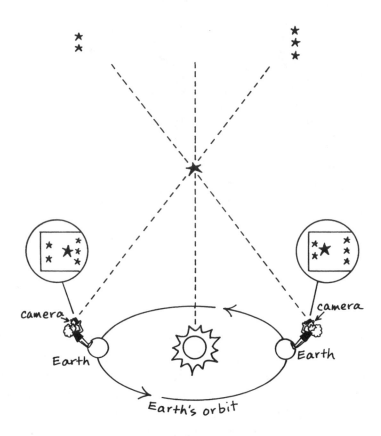

Because of the great distance of the stars from Earth, the parallax of even the closest stars is very slight. Earlier astronomers did not have the instruments necessary to make these small measurements. The parallax of a star was first measured in 1838 by Friedrich Bessel (1784–1846), a German astronomer. Today, with more precise measuring instruments and good photographic equipment and spacecraft, the parallax of many thousands of stars has been measured.

Let's Think It Through

1. Light travels from a star through space toward Earth. The star **Pollux** (PAH-luks) in the constellation **Gemini** (JEH-muh-nye) is 36 ly from Earth. Imagine the light that left this star on the day you were born. How old will you be when you see this light?

2. Which set of diagrams—A or B—represents parallax?

A

B

Answers

1. *Think!*

- How long does it take the light from Pollux to travel to Earth? Thirty-six years.

You will be 36 years old when you see the light that left Pollux on the day you were born.

2. *Think!*

- Parallax is the apparent shift of an object when viewed from different positions.

- With parallax, a different background appears behind the object viewed.

- Which set of diagrams shows the child in front of a different background?

Diagram B represents parallax.

Exercises

Use the diagrams of the zodiac constellations and the Star Distances chart to answer the following:

1. Which star shown is closest to Earth?

2. In the constellations shown, which contains the star that is farthest away?

STAR DISTANCES

Star	Distance from Earth (in ly)
Antares	325
Castor	46
Pollux	36
Spica	260

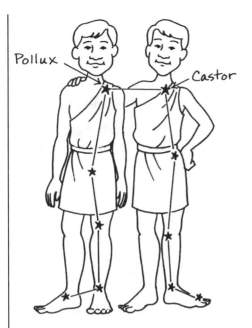

GEMINI, THE TWINS

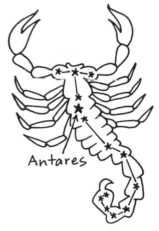

SCORPIUS,
THE SCORPION

VIRGO, THE MAIDEN

Activity: SHIFTING

Purpose   To demonstrate the effect of distance on parallax.

Materials   3-foot (1-m) strip of adding-machine paper
marking pen
masking tape
pencil

Procedure

1. Fold the adding-machine paper in half four times.

2. Unfold the paper, draw an arrow on the center fold, and number the folds 1 through 7 on each side of the arrow as shown.

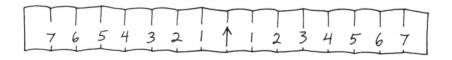

3. Tape the paper to a wall at about eye level.

4. Stand in front of the arrow, then walk backward six steps.

5. Hold the pencil upright in front of, but not touching, your nose. The top of the pencil should be about even with the top of your eyes.

6. Close your left eye and notice the mark on the paper that the pencil appears to be in line with or closest to.

7. Without moving your head or the pencil, open your left eye and close your right eye. Notice the mark on the paper that the pencil appears to be in line with or closest to.

8. Repeat steps 5 through 7, holding the pencil at arm's length.

Results   The pencil first appears to move toward the left then toward the right. This movement is less when the pencil is held at a distance from your face.

Why?   Parallax is the apparent shift in the position of any object when it is viewed from different places. Each of your eyes views the pencil from a different angle. Thus, the background for the pencil is different for each eye. The closer the pencil is to your eyes, the greater the angle formed between the eyes and the pencil. This large angle causes a large parallax when the pencil is viewed by each eye in turn. The farther the pencil is from your eyes, the smaller the angle between the eyes and the pencil, and thus the smaller the parallax.

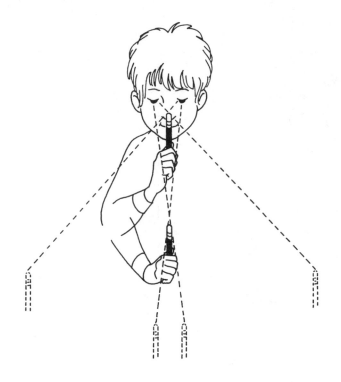

Solutions to Exercises

1.   *Think!*

- Which star in the chart is the fewest light-years from Earth?

  Pollux is the closest star shown.

2.   *Think!*

- Which star in the chart is the most light-years from Earth? Antares.

- Which constellation is Antares in?

  Of the three constellations—Gemini, Scorpius, and Virgo—Scorpius contains the star that is farthest from Earth.

15
Star Bright
How the Brightness of Stars Is Compared

What You Need to Know

The stars in some constellations all seem to shine with the same brightness, while stars in other constellations may not shine with the same brightness. Some may be very bright, others barely visible, and the rest somewhere in between. Star maps generally use size to indicate brightness, although the size of a star on a map does not indicate the actual size of the star. The brightest stars are the largest on the map, and the faintest stars are the smallest.

The diagram shows some stars in the constellation Taurus, the Bull. The different sizes of dots indicate the different brightnesses of the stars. **Aldebaran** (al-DEH-buh-run) is the brightest star. Thus, Aldebaran is represented in the diagram as the largest dot. **El Nath** (el NATH) is the next brightest star, as shown by a smaller dot. The difference in brightness of the remaining stars is less obvious. Some are brighter than others, but for most there is little difference in brightness. Thus, there is little difference in the size of the dots.

Over 2,000 years ago, the Greek astronomer Hipparchus of Nicaea (c. 190–120 B.C.) designed a system for identifying stars according to their **apparent brightness** (how bright a celestial object appears to be as observed from Earth). He assigned numbers 1 through 6 to the stars to indicate brightness. The brightest stars were assigned magnitude 1; the faintest stars that can be

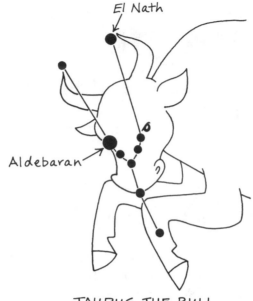

El Nath

Aldebaran

TAURUS, THE BULL

seen with the naked eye (with perfect viewing conditions) were assigned magnitude 6. This measurement of a celestial object's apparent brightness is called its **apparent magnitude**.

On the modern **apparent magnitude scale** (a list of apparent magnitudes), a first-magnitude star is exactly 100 times brighter than a sixth-magnitude star. This scale also measures magnitudes greater than 6 and less than 1. The brightest star, besides the Sun, is **Sirius** (SIHR-ee-us), which has a magnitude of −1.5. With aids such as the telescope, stars fainter than magnitude 6 are now visible. The diagram of the constellation Aries, the Ram, shows the magnitudes of the stars in parentheses. As indicated by their lower numbers, the stars **Hamal** (huh-MAHL) and **Sheratan** (SHER-uh-tun) are brighter than **Mesarthim** (MEZ-ar-thim).

There is a difference between the apparent brightness of a star and its **luminosity** (the quantity of light given off). Luminosity depends on how much light energy enters the observer's eye each second. The apparent brightness of stars depends not only on their luminosity but also on their distance from Earth. Some stars

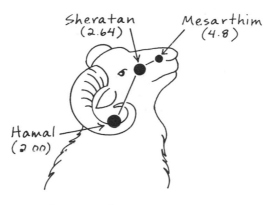

Sheratan
(2.64)

Mesarthim
(4.8)

Hamal
(2.00)

ARIES, THE RAM

are very large, such as Aldebaran in the constellation Taurus, which is about 35 times larger than the Sun. Aldebaran is about 100 times as luminous as the Sun, but because it is so far away, it appears less bright than does the Sun. Aldebaran's apparent magnitude is only 0.9 compared to −26.8 for the Sun. If two stars have the same magnitude, the more distant star has the greater luminosity. When two stars have the same luminosity, the closer star appears brighter and therefore has the lower apparent magnitude.

The light from a star spreads out uniformly in all directions. The amount of light energy reaching Earth decreases as the distance to the star increases. The following diagram shows how light spreads from stars at three different distances from Earth. The lines in the boxes at the right of the diagram represent the brightness seen from an observer on Earth. All three stars have the same luminosity, as indicated by the same number of lines (6) in the boxes. The star at distance 1 appears the brightest, as indicated by the closeness of the lines, while the one at distance 3 appears the faintest, as indicated by the separation of the lines.

Astronomers also use a measure of luminosity called **absolute magnitude** to compare the brightness of stars. This system measures the brightness of stars as if they were all placed at a distance of 32.6 ly from Earth. With this system, the Sun would not appear to be our brightest star. The Sun's absolute magnitude is about 5; that of Aldebaran and the most luminous stars, about –6. Thus, if the Sun and Aldebaran were both about 32.6 ly from Earth, the Sun would not be as bright as Aldebaran. Apparent magnitude is more commonly used than absolute magnitude. Thus, all the magnitudes given in this book are apparent magnitudes.

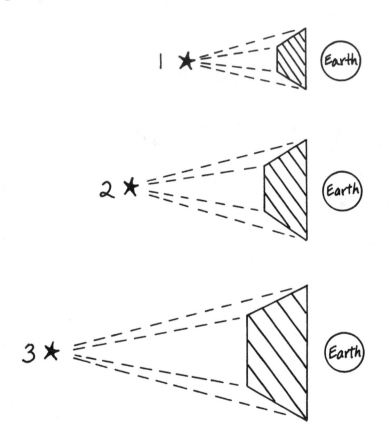

Let's Think It Through

The diagram shows the apparent magnitudes of the stars in the constellation **Cygnus** (SIG-nus), the Swan. Study the diagram and list the stars—A through F—in order of their magnitude from brightest to faintest.

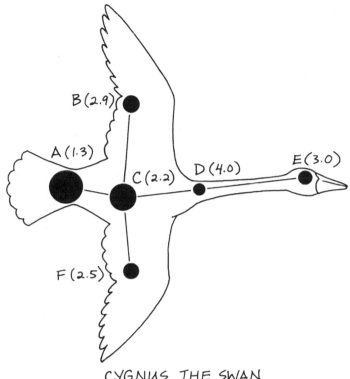

CYGNUS, THE SWAN

Answers

Think!

- The lower the magnitude, the brighter the star.
- Which star has the lowest magnitude? Star A.

  The stars in order from brightest to faintest are A, C, F, B, E, and D.

Exercises

Study the Star Brightness chart to answer the following:

1. Which is the faintest star in the chart?

2. Which star, Antares in Scorpius or **Spica** (SPY-kuh) in Virgo, has the greater luminosity?

STAR BRIGHTNESS

Star	Constellation	Apparent Magnitude	Distance from Earth (in ly)
Alrisha	Pisces	+3.8	98.0
Antares	Scorpius	+1.0	325.0
Denebola	Leo	+2.14	39.0
Pollux	Gemini	+1.1	36.0
Spica	Virgo	+1.0	260.0
Sun	—	–26.8	0.00002

3. The flashlights in the diagram represent two stars. Let the number of circles in each spot of light on the wall indicate luminosity. Study the diagram to determine which flashlight—A or B—represents the brighter star.

Activity: SPREADING

Purpose   To demonstrate how a star's distance affects its apparent magnitude.

Materials   2 identical incandescent flashlights with new batteries
yardstick (meterstick)
2 helpers

NOTE: This experiment must be performed outdoors after dark.

Procedure

1. Ask your helpers to stand side by side.

2. Turn the flashlights on and have each helper hold one.

3. Stand about 10 feet (3 m) in front of your helpers.

4. Instruct your helpers to point the lights toward your face.

5. Look at the lights just long enough to compare their brightness.

CAUTION: Do not stare at the lights.

6. Ask one of your helpers to move about 30 feet (9 m) or more from you while continuing to point the light toward you.

7. Again, compare the brightness of the lights.

Results   The brightness of the lights appears to be the same when they are at the same distance from you. When they are at different distances, the closer light looks brighter.

Why?   The light from the flashlights represents the light from two stars that give off the same amount of light. The light spreads out uniformly in all directions from the flashlights, as it does from stars. The spreading of light from more distant stars results in less light reaching Earth. Thus, two stars with the same luminosity, but at different distances from Earth, will appear to have different apparent magnitudes.

Solutions to Exercises

1. *Think!*

   • The higher the magnitude, the fainter the star.

   • Which star in the chart has the highest magnitude?

   Alrisha (al-RISH-uh), in the constellation Pisces, is the faintest star in the chart.

2. *Think!*

   • Both Antares and Spica have the same magnitude. Thus, from Earth their brightness appears to be equal.

- When two stars have the same apparent magnitude, the more distant star has the greater luminosity.

- Which star is farther away?

  Antares is the more luminous star.

3. *Think!*

- Both lights have 5 circles, thus both have the same luminosity.

- When two stars have the same luminosity, the closer star appears brighter.

- Which flashlight represents the closer star?

  Flashlight B represents the brighter star.

16
Springtime Patterns
Locating the Spring Constellations

What You Need to Know

Different constellations can best be viewed at different times of year. The spring constellations are those easiest to see from late March through early June. This chapter and chapter 18, "The Sea Monster," show how to find some of the spring constellations, and the star maps indicate good viewing dates and times. Remember, when using a star map for an earlier date or time than those on the map, the constellations will be more toward the east. For later dates and times, they will be more toward the west.

The spring zodiac constellations and good visible dates are Cancer, in March, Leo in April, Virgo in May, and Libra in June. There are more first-magnitude stars visible in the spring than any other season. Two of the zodiac constellations, Leo and Virgo, along with late spring constellation **Boötes** (boh-OH-teez), the Herdsman, contain at least one of these bright stars. Although Boötes is called the Herdsman, its star pattern looks more like a kite. At latitudes 40°N or greater, the northern circumpolar constellation most visible during the spring is Ursa Major, which is better known for its asterism, the Big Dipper.

Use the star map to find these constellations in the spring. Begin by facing north and locating the Big Dipper near your zenith. Use the two stars at the back of the bowl, Megrez and Phecda, to find

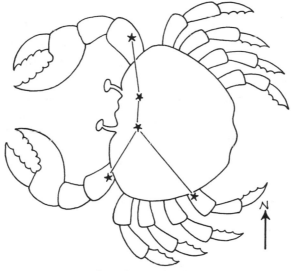

CANCER, THE CRAB

BOÖTES, THE HERDSMAN

Leo. Starting at Megrez, follow a line from these two stars toward Regulus, the brightest star in Leo. From Regulus, face west and follow a line northwestward to a pair of bright stars. These are **Castor** (KAS-tur) and Pollux in the constellation Gemini. Gemini is considered a winter constellation and can best be seen in February, but it is still very visible in the western sky in early spring. Between Leo and Gemini is the constellation Cancer, made up of five faint stars.

Return to the Big Dipper. Follow the curve of the dipper's handle outward to **Arcturus** (ark-TUR-us), the brightest star in the constellation Boötes. East of Boötes is the U-shaped constellation Corona Borealis. To find the constellation Virgo, return to

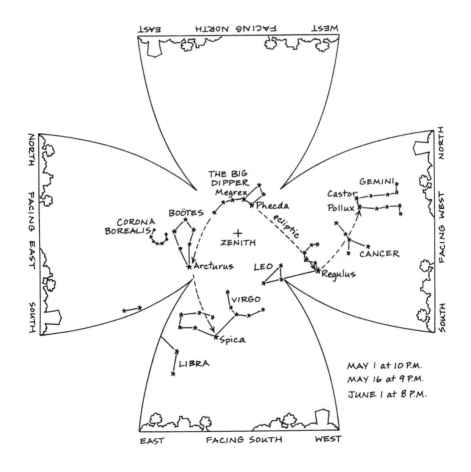

Arcturus and follow a curved line past Arcturus to Spica, the brightest star in Virgo. Libra can be found by looking southeast of Spica. Like Cancer, Libra is made up of faint stars, so it is difficult to find.

The measurements called azimuth and altitude are used to describe where a constellation appears in the sky. The **azimuth** of an object is its distance in degrees clockwise around the horizon from north. At due north, the azimuth is 0°. At due east, it is 90° from north. At due south, it is 180° from north. At due west, it is 270° from north.

The **altitude** of an object is its height above the horizon. Altitude, like azimuth, is measured in degrees. At any place along the horizon, the altitude is 0°. At the zenith, the altitude is 90°. Since constellations contain several stars with different azimuths and altitudes, a single azimuth or altitude is not given for a constellation. Instead, the azimuth and altitude for a star in the constellation can be used to locate the star and thus the constellation. The diagram shows a star with an azimuth of 40° and an altitude of 25°. Thus, to find this star, face northeast and look about one-fourth of the way between the horizon and the zenith.

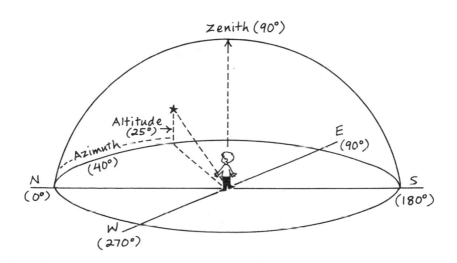

Let's Think It Through

Study the diagram and use one or more of these names to answer the following questions: Arcturus, the Big Dipper, Boötes, Leo, Regulus.

1. What is the name of star A?

2. What is the name of the constellation that star B is a part of?

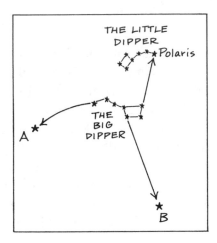

Answers

1.   *Think!*

• An imaginary curved line drawn from the Big Dipper's handle leads to which of the bright stars?

Star A is Arcturus in the constellation Boötes.

2.   *Think!*

• A line extended from the two stars at the back of the Big Dipper's bowl leads to which of the bright stars? Regulus.

• Which constellation is Regulus a part of?

Star B is in the constellation Leo.

Exercises

Use the constellation diagrams to answer the following questions:

1. Identify the constellations represented by each figure—1, 2, 3, and 4.

2. Which location on the map—A, B, C, or D—is the place to look for a winter constellation that can be seen in early spring?

3. Which location on the map—A, B, C, or D—is the place to look for Virgo?

4. Where would you look for the constellation Gemini when Castor has an azimuth of 270° and an altitude of 50°?

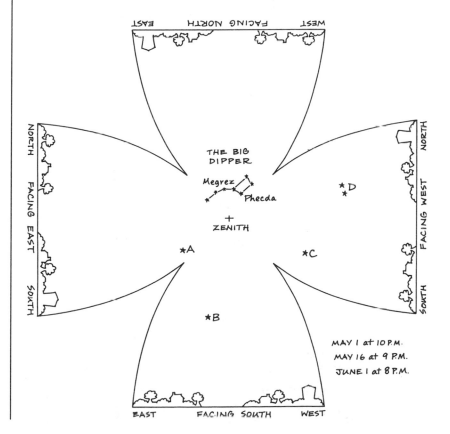

Activity: STAR HEIGHTS

Purpose To measure the azimuth and altitude of a star.

Materials protractor
marking pen
premium-strength paper dinner plate
cardboard tube from a paper towel roll
scissors
masking tape
drinking straw
pushpin

directional compass
astronomer's flashlight from chapter 4
adult helper

Procedure

1. Construct the **compass rose** (an instrument used to measure azimuth) by following these steps:

    *   Use the protractor and pen to mark every 10° around the paper plate as shown, starting with 0°. Label 0°N, 90°E, 180°S, and 270°W.

    *   Stand the tube in the center of the plate and draw around it.

    *   Cut out the circle you drew, so that the hole is big enough for the tube to stand in snugly but still turn freely.

COMPASS ROSE

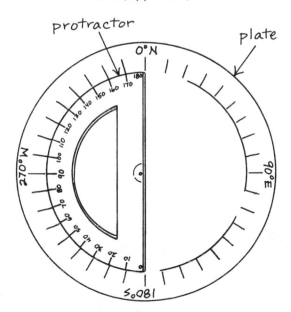

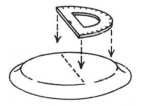

2. Construct the astrolabe by following these steps:

- Turn the protractor upside down. Without covering the lines, cover the numbers on the left side of the protractor with small pieces of tape.

- Write 0° to 90° on the pieces of tape as shown in the diagram.

- Center the straw along the straight edge of the protractor and secure it with tape.

- Fasten the protractor to the approximate center of the tube by inserting the pushpin through the center hole in the straight edge of the protractor and into the tube.

- Place the compass rose on a table outdoors and stand the tube in the hole of the compass rose.

- Hold the protractor so that the straw is perpendicular to the tube. Point the straw toward the horizon in any direction.

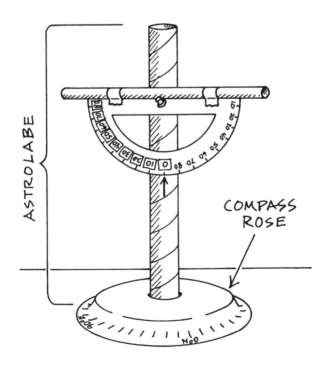

- Close one eye and look through the straw with your open eye. If you cannot see the horizon through the straw, then adjust the height of the protractor on the tube.

- Mark an arrow on the tube below the 0° mark taped on the protractor. You have made an astrolabe.

3. At night, go outdoors and place the astrolabe on the edge of a table. Use the compass to position the compass rose so that 0° points due north.

4. Tape the compass rose to the table in this position.

5. Holding the end of the straw that is near you and keeping one eye closed, look through the straw and search for a star. Slowly push down on the end of the straw to see above the horizon.

6. Ask your helper to use the flashlight first to read the angle on the protractor as indicated by the arrow on the tube and

then to look at the compass rose to determine the direction the straw is pointing.

7. Repeat steps 5 and 6, locating several stars within a single constellation, such as Leo.

Results The higher the selected star is above the horizon, the greater the angle. As the tube is turned, the astrolabe points to a different part of the horizon.

Why? An **astrolabe** is an instrument that is used to measure altitude. When the altitude is 0°, the straw of the astrolabe points toward the horizon. When you raise the end of the straw in order to see a star at a higher altitude, the protractor rotates on the pushpin. As the end of the protractor rotates upward, the arrow on the tube indicates increasingly greater angles. As the tube is turned, the astrolabe points to the star's azimuth as indicated by the compass rose.

Solutions to Exercises

1. **Think!**

   • Which constellation looks like a lion? Leo

   • Which constellation looks like a herdsman? Boötes

   • Which constellation looks like twin boys? Gemini

   • Which constellation looks like a young maiden? Virgo

     The names of the constellation represented by each figure are: Leo-1, Boötes-2, Gemini-3, and Virgo-4.

2. **Think!**

   • Which is a winter constellation seen in early spring? Gemini.

   • Where is Gemini located? To the west of Leo.

- An imaginary line drawn from the stars Megrez and Phecda in the bowl of the Big Dipper leads to Leo at location C.

- From Regulus, the brightest star in Leo, one looks northwest to find Gemini.

The winter constellation Gemini can be seen at location D during early spring.

3. ***Think!***

- To find Virgo, first locate Boötes.

- Follow a curved line from the end of the Big Dipper's handle to Arcturus in the constellation Boötes at location A.

- Continue the curved line from Arcturus to Spica in the constellation Virgo.

Virgo is at location B.

4. ***Think!***

- The azimuth tells the observer which horizon to face. An azimuth of 270° is due west.

- The altitude describes how far above the horizon a star is. At the zenith, the altitude is 90°. Halfway between the horizon and the zenith, the altitude is 45°.

When Castor has an azimuth of 270° and an altitude of 50°, Gemini can be found by facing due west and looking a little higher than halfway between the horizon and the zenith.

17
The Sea Monster

Locating the Constellation Hydra

What You Need to Know

Hydra (HYE-druh), the Sea Monster, is seen in an imaginary ocean in a very barren part of the sky. During the spring, this fictitious monster swims across the southern sky from low in the southeast to high in the southwest. From head to tail, Hydra reaches about one-third of the way around the sky, making it the longest constellation.

Even though it is very large, Hydra is not the most noticeable constellation in the springtime sky. It contains only one bright star, **Alphard** (AL-fard), with a magnitude of about 2. All the

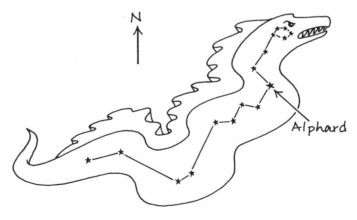

HYDRA, THE SEA MONSTER

other stars are magnitude 3 or greater. Since there are no other bright stars and very few stars of any brightness around Alphard, it has been nicknamed the Solitary One.

Using the star map to find Hydra in the spring, first use Megrez and Phecda in the Big Dipper to find Regulus in Leo, then continue the line toward a bright star. This star is Alphard in Hydra. The head, lying to the west of Alphard below Cancer, is the most sea monster–like part of the star pattern. The head is more easily found than the rest of the body, which winds its way across the sky below the constellations Leo and Virgo.

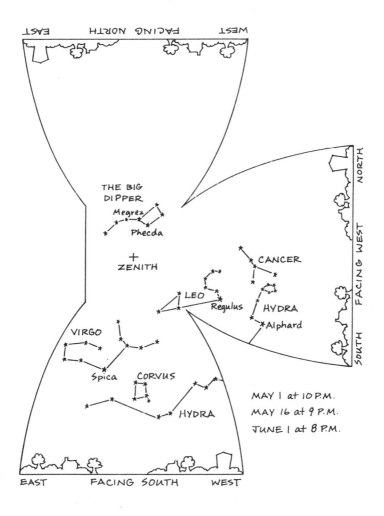

Southwest of the star Spica in Virgo and on the lower back of Hydra appears to ride the constellation **Corvus** (KOR-vus), the Crow. The four main stars of Corvus's body are easily seen because, even though their magnitudes range from about 2.5 to 3, there are no other bright stars nearby. Corvus might be imagined as pecking at Hydra's back.

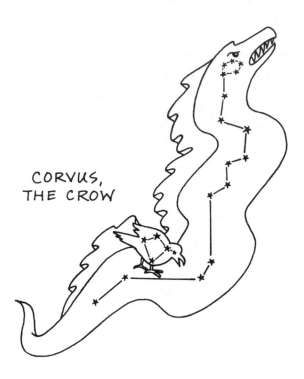

CORVUS,
THE CROW

Let's Think It Through

Study the diagram on the next page and determine which arrow—A, B, C, or D—points toward Hydra.

Answer

Think!

- Hydra can be found by following an imaginary line from Megrez and Phecda in the back of the Big Dipper's bowl through Regulus to Alphard in Hydra.

Arrow D points toward Hydra.

Exercises

Study the diagram and determine which position—A, B, C, or D—represents the location of the following constellations:

1. Corvus

2. Leo

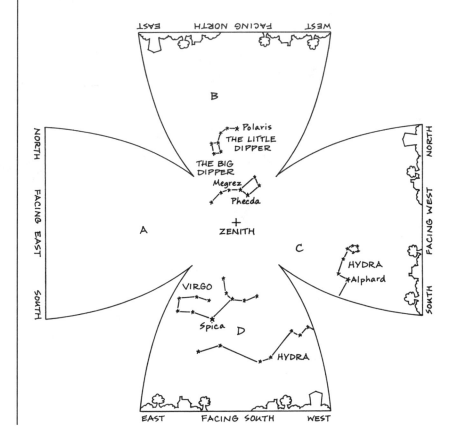

Activity: WHICH WAY?

Purpose   To determine the visible length of Hydra for a specific date and time.

Materials   astrolabe from chapter 16
directional compass
masking tape
astronomer's flashlight from chapter 4
pencil
paper

Procedure

1. Set the astrolabe near the edge of a table outdoors.

2. Lay the compass next to the compass rose. Turn the compass rose so that its 0°N mark points north. Tape the compass rose to the table in this position.

3. Look at the sky and find the head of Hydra.

4. Turn the tube of the astrolabe and point the straw toward Hydra's head.

5. Look through the straw, keeping one eye closed. As you look through the straw, rotate the tube of the astrolabe to find the most westerly star in the head of Hydra.

6. Without moving the astrolabe, ask a helper to use the flashlight to read and record the degree mark on the compass rose. This is the azimuth reading.

7. Repeat steps 3 through 6 to find the most easterly star in the tail of Hydra.

8. Calculate the visible length of Hydra by subtracting the smaller azimuth reading for the tail from the larger azimuth reading for the head.

9. Repeat this activity on other dates and times.

Results   From head to tail, the length of Hydra is about 120°.

Why?   Hydra's stars appear to move in a westward direction across the sky, but the apparent distance between the stars does not change. Thus, the visible length of Hydra remains the same regardless of the date or time. (Note that due to visibility problems, such as light from the Moon, houses, or cars; clouds in the way; or the constellation's nearness to the horizon, all of the constellation may not be visible.)

Solutions to Exercises

1. *Think!*

   • Corvus is southwest of Spica in Virgo and at the far end
     of Hydra's back.

   Corvus is at location D.

2. *Think!*

   • Leo lies generally between the star Alphard in Hydra
     and the stars Megrez and Phecda in the Big Dipper.

   Leo is at location C.

18
Summertime Patterns

Locating the Summer Constellations

What You Need to Know

Summer constellations are those that are easiest to see from late June through early September. The summer constellations do not have as many first-magnitude stars as do the spring constellations. However, there are many constellations to see, and the weather should allow you to spend a longer time studying the sky.

Calling a constellation a seasonal constellation doesn't mean it is only seen during the months of that season. The constellations continually parade across the sky from one season to the next. While the spring constellations were making their way from east to west across the southern sky, the summer constellations were rising in the east and following them. At the beginning of a season, such as summer, some of the constellations of late spring can still be seen. This is true for Boötes and **Corona Borealis** (kuh-ROH-nuh bor-ee-A-lus), the Northern Crown, which, along with the summer constellations Draco, Lyra, Cygnus, and Hercules, spend most of the summer high overhead near the zenith. **Aquila** (A-kwuh-luh), the Eagle, is nearer the horizon, but it is a distinctive summer constellation.

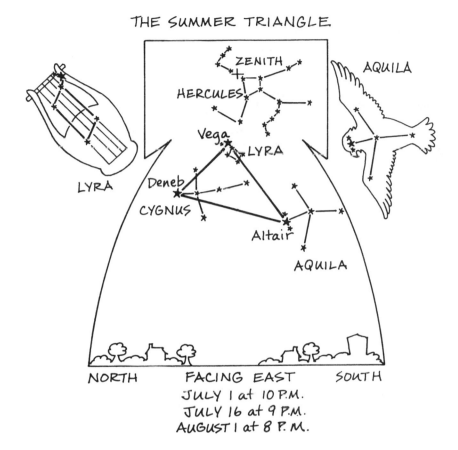

THE SUMMER TRIANGLE

Imaginary lines between three very bright stars—Vega in Lyra, **Deneb** (DEH-neb) in Cygnus, and **Altair** (al-TYRE) in Aquila—form what is called the Summer Triangle. Using the star map, the triangle can be found by facing east. Vega is the brightest of the three stars and can be located high overhead and below Hercules. Draw a line toward the northeast horizon to find Deneb. Return to Vega and follow a line toward the southeast horizon to Altair. Once you have located all three stars, you can imagine the connecting lines that form the triangle.

All the summertime zodiac constellations except Ophiuchus are found near the horizon. Using the map, the zodiac constellations are located by facing south. Ophiuchus is found by looking below Hercules. Libra, Scorpius, and Sagittarius are near the southern horizon. Leo and Virgo are near the western horizon and are not visible above the horizon all summer. Capricornus is near the eastern horizon, and Aquarius is rising above the eastern horizon.

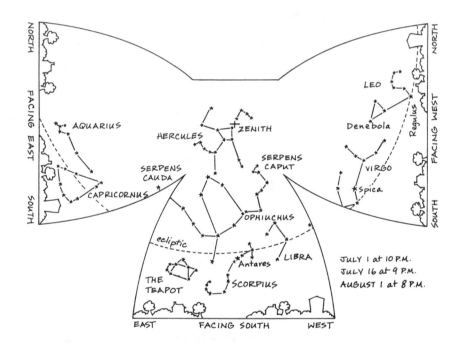

Let's Think It Through

Study the map diagram on the following page and use previous star maps in this chapter to determine which triangle—A, B, or C—represents the location of the Summer Triangle on the dates and times shown.

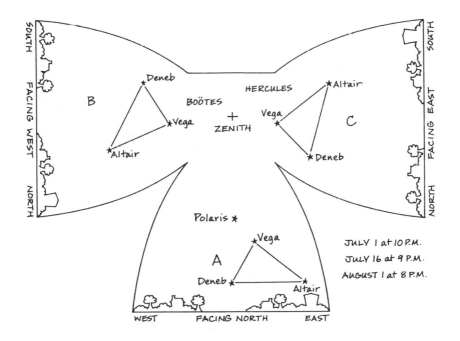

Answers

- The Summer Triangle is made by connecting three bright stars—Vega, Deneb, and Altair.

- Vega is near zenith and east of Hercules.

- On the map, the stars in the Summer Triangle are found in the eastern sky.

  Triangle C represents the location of the Summer Triangle in early summer.

Exercise

Study the diagrams and choose the constellation that has a star in the Summer Triangle.

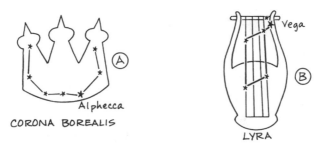

CORONA BOREALIS

LYRA

Activity: BRIGHTER

Purpose To model the collection of starlight by a refractive telescope.

Materials sheet of typing paper
magnifying lens

Procedure

1. In a darkened room, stand facing away and as far as possible from a window.

2. Hold the paper to one side with one hand.

3. With your other hand, hold the magnifying lens between the paper and the window so that the lens is near, but not touching, the paper.

4. Move the lens toward or away from the paper until you see a clear image on the paper.

Result   A small, inverted image of the window and objects outside the window is projected onto the paper.

Why?   Many stars in the summer constellations, or in the constellations of any season, are difficult if not impossible to see with the naked eye. A **telescope** (an instrument that makes far-off objects appear closer and larger) is used to make these more visible. The magnifying lens used in this experiment and the **objective lens** in the large end of a **refractive telescope** (a telescope with two lenses, an objective lens and an eyepiece) are convex lenses. **Convex lenses** are transparent, curved structures that are thicker in the center than at the edges. Light rays passing through a convex lens are **refracted** (bent) toward a **focal point** (a point where refracted light rays **converge** or come together). With the magnifying lens, the image is produced at a point past the focal point, but with the refractive telescope, because the light is coming from such a long distance, the image is at the focal point. Both images are smaller than the object being viewed and upside down. The telescope has a second convex lens, the **eyepiece** (the lens closest to the eye), which **magnifies** (makes larger) the image produced by the objective lens.

REFRACTIVE TELESCOPE

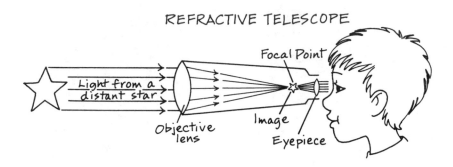

Solution to Exercise

Think!

• Which stars make up the Summer Triangle? Vega in Lyra, Deneb in Cygnus, and Altair in Aquila.

Lyra, constellation B, has a star in the Summer Triangle.

19
The Kneeler

Locating the Constellation Hercules

What You Need to Know

Hercules, the Kneeler, is a large summer constellation. The stars of this sky pattern are most visible during the summer, but even then they are dim. It takes some imagination to see a man kneeling on his right knee with a club in one hand and a bow and arrow in the other, especially because the fearless warrior imagined in Hercules stands on his head as he moves across the southern sky. The lowest star is **Rasalgethi** (raz-ul-GEE-thee), in Hercules's head. Above Rasalgethi is a four-sided figure

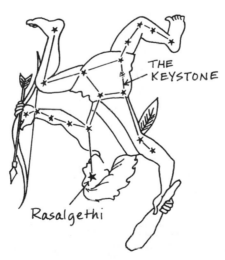

HERCULES, THE KNEELER

called the Keystone. The four corner stars of this asterism mark Hercules's lower body.

Using the star map, one way to locate Hercules is to face west and locate the star Arcturus in Boötes overhead. Follow an imaginary line east past Corona Borealis (see chapter 18) to the faint stars making up the shape of a kneeling warrior. Look for the four stars of the Keystone that form Hercules's lower body. The stars forming his arms extend toward the southern horizon, and his legs are toward the north.

Another method of finding Hercules is to locate the head of Draco near the zenith (see chapter 10). Hercules's left foot appears to rest on the head of the dragon, and he is facing east, toward Aquila in the Summer Triangle (see chapter 18).

The most outstanding features of Hercules are the red supergiant star Rasalgethi and two spectacular **globular clusters,** (cluster of several tens of thousands to maybe 1 million stars). The globular clusters are called M13 and M92. Rasalgethi is a variable star. The name is Arabic for "the kneeler's head." The star's magnitude ranges from about 3 to 4 and makes this change over a period of about 90 to 100 days. The change is slow but can be observed with the naked eye. It is a very large star, having a diameter several hundreds of times the diameter of the Sun. It does not appear to be very large in the sky because it is 220 ly away from Earth. Its dimness is also due to its being relatively cool, having a surface temperature below 5400°F (3000°C) as compared to the Sun, which is almost twice as hot. (See chapter 23 for more information about the surface temperatures of stars.)

On the star map, between the two stars on the western side of the Keystone is a smudge of light. This is the globular cluster M13. This is the brightest globular cluster north of the celestial equator. It is just barely visible with the naked eye on a clear, moonless night. In 1715, Edmond Halley (1656–1742), an English astronomer, first observed the cluster, describing it as a "little patch." Later, English astronomer William Herschel

(1738–1822) estimated M13 to contain about 14,000 stars. With more precise instruments to study the cluster, astronomers today consider the number of stars to be closer to a half million. Like all globular clusters, M13 is very far away, at a distance of about 23,000 ly. The globular cluster M92 is much farther away, at a distance of 37,000 ly. M92 lies north of the Keystone, between Hercules's knees. Very keen eyes are needed to see M92 with the naked eye, but with a telescope it appears similar to M13 but with a larger number of variable stars.

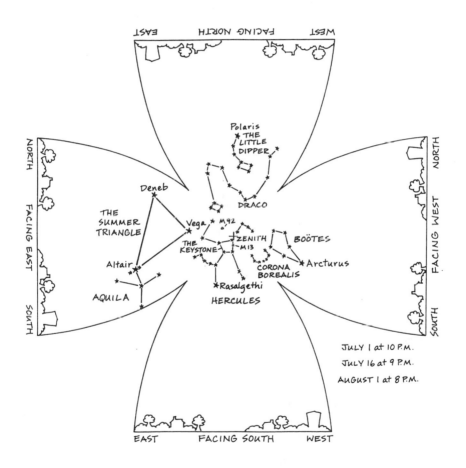

JULY 1 at 10 P.M.
JULY 16 at 9 P.M.
AUGUST 1 at 8 P.M.

Let's Think It Through

Study the diagrams and choose the one—A, B, or C—that when facing south represents the position of the constellation Hercules during the summer.

Answers

Think!

- Diagram A shows a boy standing. Hercules kneels in the sky, like diagrams B and C.

- During the summer, Hercules is upside down.

  Diagram C represents the position of the constellation Hercules during the summer.

Exercises

Study the star diagram of Hercules and answer the following:

1. Which position—A, B, C, D, or E—is the location of Rasalgethi, "the kneeler's head"?

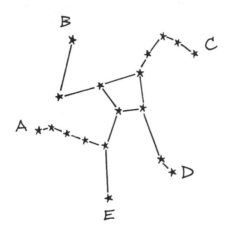

EAST   FACING SOUTH   WEST

2. Which position—A, B, C, D, or E—is the location of the star closest to the head of Draco?

Activity: BRIGHTER

Purpose   To demonstrate how the faint stars and globular clusters of Hercules can be made more visible.

Materials   2 sheets of typing paper
transparent tape
ruler
measuring cup
2 cups of rice
2 large bowls
helper

Procedure

1. Roll each paper into a cone and secure with tape. Make one cone about 1 inch (2.5 cm) in diameter across the opening, and the other about 6 inches (15 cm) in diameter.

2. Place 1 cup (250 ml) of rice in one of the large bowls.

3. Set the empty bowl on the ground outdoors. A grassy area works well.

4. Ask your helper to hold the smaller cone open end up in the empty bowl.

5. Holding the bowl of rice about 3 feet (1 m) above the opening in the cone, pour the rice into the cone.

6. Use the measuring cup to measure the amount of rice that falls into the cone.

7. Repeat steps 2 through 6, using the larger cone.

Results   More rice is caught by the larger cone.

Why?   Refractive telescopes used to study the stars of Hercules or any other constellation have one large end and one small end. The large end, directed toward the sky, has an objective lens that collects large quantities of light, just as the large cone collects large quantities of rice. The small end of the telescope has an eyepiece. This second lens magnifies the star images received by the objective lens. Larger objective lenses collect more light and produce brighter images of the stars.

Solutions to Exercises

1. *Think!*

   - Hercules is upside down in the sky. Which stars are lowest? D and E.

   - His right arm faces west and his head faces east. Which star, D or E, faces east?

   Position E is the location of Rasalgethi.

2. *Think!*

   - Hercules's left foot appears to rest on the head of Draco.

   - If position D shows Hercules's right arm, which star marks his left foot?

   Position B is the location of the star closest to Draco's head.

20
Autumn
Patterns

Locating the Autumn Constellations

What You Need to Know

Autumn constellations are those that are easiest to see from late September through early December. Some of these are Cassiopeia, the Queen; Cepheus, the King; **Pegasus** (PEH-guh-sus), the Winged Horse; Andromeda, the Princess; and **Perseus** (PUR-sus), the Hero. The autumn constellations overlap and are not as clear as those in the spring and summer. Nevertheless, there are interesting star patterns.

High overhead in autumn can be seen the four stars that make up the Great Square. Like the Summer Triangle in the summer sky, the Great Square is one of the featured attractions in the autumn sky. The Diamond would be a more accurate name. The four-sided geometric shape might lead some modern sky observers to see it as a baseball diamond. The Great Square, like the Summer Triangle, is a combination of stars. Three of the four stars forming the square—**Scheat** (SHEE-at), **Markab** (MAR-kab), and **Algenib** (al-JEE-nib)—belong to the constellation Pegasus. The fourth star, **Alpheratz** (al-FEE-rats), is in Andromeda.

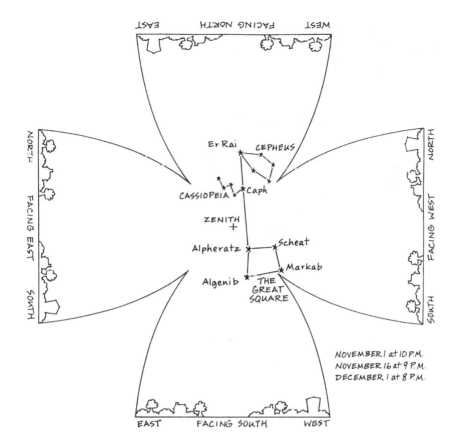

Using the star map to find the Great Square, first locate the constellations Cassiopeia and Cepheus, which are most visible high in the northern sky in autumn (see chapters 8 and 9). Two stars, Caph in Cassiopeia and Er Rai in Cepheus, can be used to find the star Alpheratz in the Great Square. Follow an imaginary line from Er Rai through Caph across the zenith to Alpheratz. (This is more comfortably done lying on your back and facing south than standing and facing north.) From Alpheratz, look west, southwest, and southeast, respectively, to find Scheat, Markab, and Algenib, the other three stars of the Great Square.

The figures of Pegasus and Andromeda are upside down in the autumn sky. Pegasus's front legs reach westward from Scheat, and its neck and head stretch southwestward from Markab. The horse's left wing extends from Algenib in the southeast. Covering the horse's hind legs is the body of a girl, Andromeda. Her

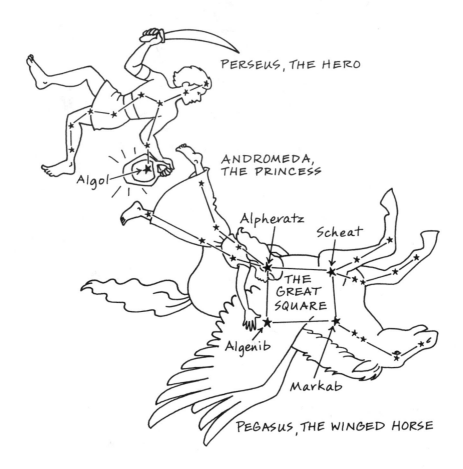

head is at Alpheratz and her legs extend northeastward. According to myth, Andromeda was rescued by the winged horse Pegasus sent by her hero, Perseus. Thus, she is seen as clinging to the horse. Perseus stands upright beyond Andromeda's feet. The blinking star **Algol** (AL-gawl) in Perseus is imagined by some to be the eye of a head held in the hero's hand, but it could also be a blinking lantern used by Perseus to watch over Andromeda. (See chapter 21 to discover why Algol blinks.)

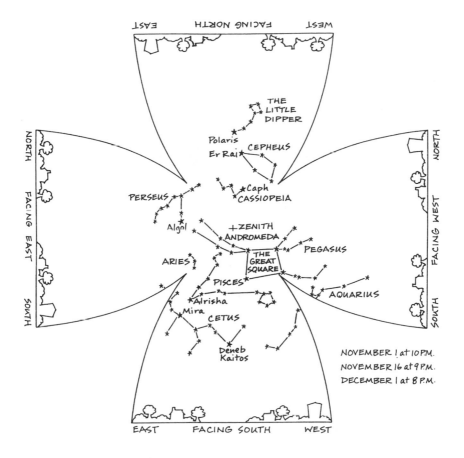

Other autumn constellations are **Cetus** (SEE-tus), the Whale, and the zodiac constellations Pisces, Aquarius, and Aries. Using the star map to find these constellations, first find Pisces.

Pisces is imagined as two fishing stringers with a fish on each end. One of the fish of Pisces is a group of stars due south of the Great Square. The knot holding the stringers together is the star **Alrisha** (al-RISH-uh) in Pisces. Southeast of Alrisha is **Mira** (MY-ruh) in Cetus. This is a variable star changing from magnitude 2 to magnitude 10 over a period of about 332 days. Mira is northeast of **Deneb Kaitos** (DEH-neb KAY-tos), the brightest star in Cetus. Return to Pisces and look west to see Aquarius, east to see Aries.

Let's Think It Through

Study the star map for November 1 at 10:00 P.M. to determine the position—A, B, C, or D—for the Great Square.

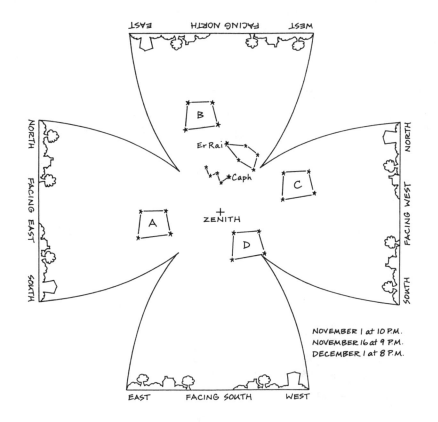

Answer

Think!

- The house-shaped constellation is Cepheus.
- The W-shaped constellation is Cassiopeia.
- A line from the star at the peak of the roof in Cepheus, Er Rai, through the most westward star in Cassiopeia, Caph, leads to the Great Square.

Position D is the location of the Great Square.

Exercise

Study the star map for November 1 at 10:00 P.M. to determine the position—A, B, C, or D—for each constellation.

1. Pisces

2. Cetus

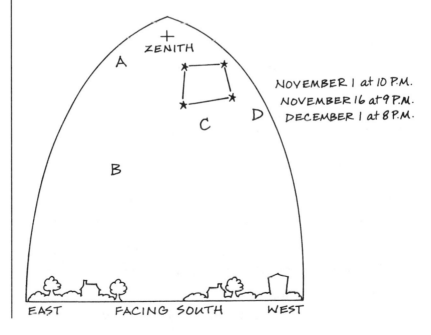

Activity: STAR BOX

Purpose   To make a star planetarium.

Materials   large shoe box with lid
scissors
ruler
flashlight
sheet of black construction paper
masking tape
tracing paper
marking pen
drawing compass

Procedure

1. Remove the lid from the box, then cut a 3-by-4-inch (7.5-by-10-cm) opening in the center of one end of the shoe box.

2. At the other end of the box, cut a circle just large enough to insert the end of the flashlight.

3. Cut a piece of black paper large enough to cover the square opening. Secure the paper to the box with tape.

4. Lay the tracing paper over the star pattern shown and trace the stars and the dots of the north directional arrow.

5. Lay the marked side of the tracing paper face down on the black paper covering the opening of the box.

6. With the pointed end of the compass, make a hole for each star and smaller holes for the dots through the tracing paper and black paper.

7. Remove the tracing paper.

8. Place a small piece of tape about 1 inch (2.5 cm) square on a blank wall at about eye level. This tape represents Polaris.

9. Put the lid on the box, then set the box on a table near the wall so that the star-patterned end faces the wall.

TOP

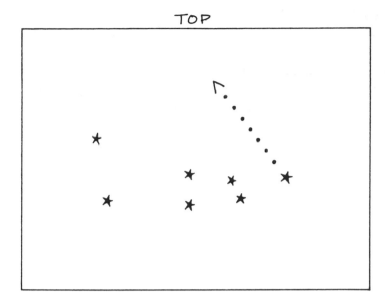

10. Insert the flashlight through the circular hole in the box.

11. Turn on the flashlight, then darken the room.

12. Move the box toward and away from the wall until clear images of small points of light appear on the wall. Make the holes in the black paper larger if the spots on the wall are too small.

13. Rotate the box so that the dots of the north directional arrow point toward the piece of tape, Polaris.

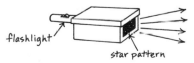

flashlight

star pattern

Results   An enlarged pattern of the holes made in the paper is projected onto the wall.

Why?   Light shining through the holes spreads out, producing larger circles of light on the wall. The stars projected on the wall are in the correct order and position as seen in the sky. The star pattern is of the constellation Andromeda.

Solutions to Exercises

1.   *Think!*

   - One of the fish of Pisces is due south of the Great Square.
   - Which position is due south of the Great Square?

   Position C is the location of Pisces.

2.   *Think!*

   - The constellation Cetus is southeast of the Great Square and below Pisces.
   - Which position is southeast of the Great Square and below Pisces at location C?

   Position B is the location of Cetus.

21
The Hero

Exploring the Constellation Perseus

What You Need to Know

Perseus is the hero who sent the winged horse Pegasus to save Andromeda, the damsel in distress (see chapter 20). The stars forming this hero are located at the feet of his lady fair. Using the star map, locate Perseus by facing north and finding the inverted W-shaped stars of Cassiopeia near the zenith in the northern sky. Follow a line east (to your right) to Perseus. Along this path is the Double Cluster, containing two star clusters that can be seen with the naked eye but are very beautiful through a telescope. Facing east, look toward the zenith to find Andromeda, which joins Pegasus high in the southwestern sky to form the Great Square.

Perseus has no first-magnitude stars, but **Mirfak** (MUR-fak), its brightest star, has a magnitude of 1.8. Another noteworthy star in Perseus is Algol. The light from this star in Perseus's left hand (see chapter 20) varies in brightness every 3 days. Algol looks like one star when viewed with the naked eye, but it is actually a binary star, two stars bound by their mutual gravity and revolving around a common point. The two stars are named Algol A and Algol B. These stars are an **eclipsing binary,** meaning that one star periodically moves in front of the other and partially or completely blocks its light. (**Eclipse** means to pass in front of and block the light of another body.)

The brighter of the two stars of a binary star pair is called a **primary star,** and the fainter star is called a **secondary star.** Algol

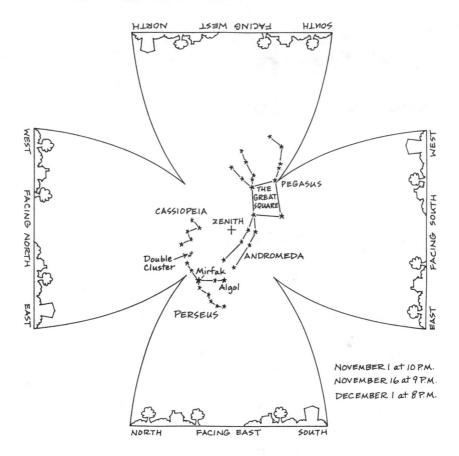

A is the primary star and Algol B the secondary star. The combination of the light from the pair when separated and when they eclipse each other makes the binary star appear to "blink" from its brightest magnitude of 2.2 to its faintest magnitude of 3.5 over a period of about 2 days and 21 hours. Most of the time the pair appears at a magnitude of 2.2, but a magnitude of 3.5 is seen when Algol B eclipses Algol A.

PERSEUS, THE HERO

Let's Think It Through

Study the star map and determine which position—A, B, or C—is the location of the Double Cluster near Perseus.

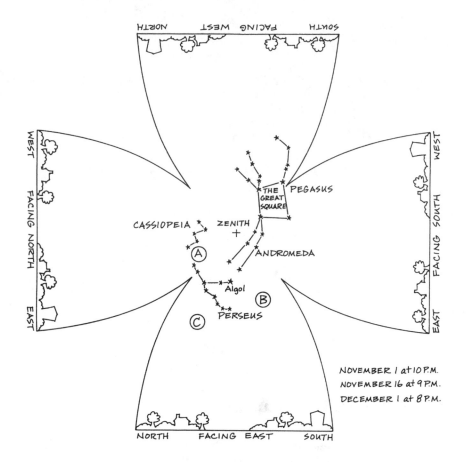

Answer

Think!

• The Double Cluster lies on a line between Cassiopeia and Perseus.

Position A is the location of the Double Cluster.

Exercises

Study the diagrams and answer the following:

1. If a lighter color indicates greater brightness, which position shows Algol A eclipsing Algol B?

2. Which position results in the faintest magnitude?

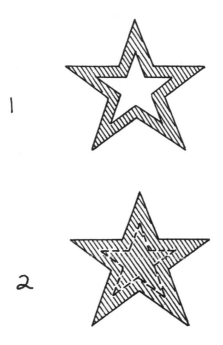

Activity: COVERUP

Purpose To demonstrate an eclipsing binary.

Materials drawing compass
sheet of typing paper
2 pencils
scissors
transparent tape

Procedure

1. Use the compass to draw a 2-inch (5-cm) and a 4-inch (10-cm) circle on the paper.

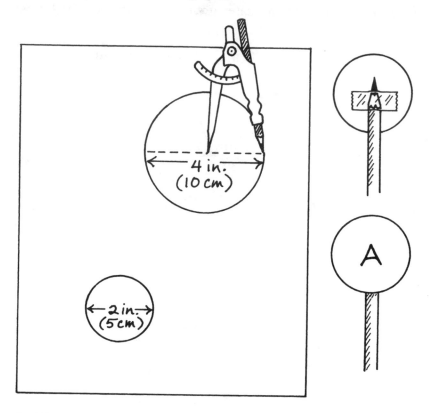

2. Use a pencil to color the larger circle.

3. Write A on the smaller circle and B on the larger circle.

4. Cut out each circle.

5. Tape a circle to the sharpened end of each pencil.

6. Hold the pencil with circle A upright about 6 to 8 inches (15 to 20 cm) in front of your face.

7. Hold the pencil with circle B upside down about 4 inches (10 cm) behind circle A.

8. Observe how much of each circle is visible.

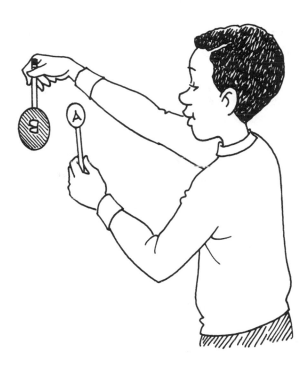

9. Move circle B around and in front of circle A.

10. Observe the visibility of each circle during this movement.

Results   When circle B is behind circle A, all of A and part of B are visible. As circle B moves around, both circles are visible for a short time, then B covers A.

Why?   The circles represent the stars Algol A and Algol B. Algol A is smaller and brighter than Algol B. The positions of these two stars are such that, seen from Earth, the stars eclipse each other. Both stars revolve around a common point, but only the orbit of Algol B is demonstrated. The eclipse of Algol B by Algol A is represented by moving circle B behind circle A. The result is that the brighter star, represented by the white paper, is in front. All the light of the brighter star and some of the light of the fainter star are seen. When the two stars are separate, the light from both is seen, producing the brightest magnitude: 2.2. The eclipse of Algol A by Algol B (when A is behind B) results in the faintest magnitude: 3.5. The light is thus fainter because the larger, fainter Algol B blocks the light from Algol A.

Solutions to Exercises

1. *Think!*

   - Algol A is a primary star, the brighter of the binary pair.
   - The smaller, brighter star in the diagrams is Algol A.
   - Eclipse means one star is in front of and blocking the light of another star.
   - Which diagram shows the brightest star in front?

   Position 1 shows Algol A eclipsing Algol B.

2. *Think!*

   - Algol B is larger and fainter than Algol A.
   - Less light is seen when Algol B eclipses Algol A.

   When Algol B is in position 2, the combination of the light from both stars results in the faintest magnitude (3.5).

22
Wintertime Patterns

Locating the Winter Constellations

What You Need to Know

Winter constellations are those that are easiest to see from late December through early March. The winter season offers more spectacular constellations than any other season. These constellations are concentrated together but include some of the brightest and easiest to locate. Winter is second only to spring for the number of first-magnitude stars. The six prominent constellations of this season are the **pentagon-shaped** (five-sided figure) **Auriga** (aw-RYE-guh), the Charioteer; Gemini, the Twins; **Canis Minor** (KAY-nus MY-nur), the Little Dog; Canis Major, the Great Dog; **Orion** (uh-RYE-un), the Hunter; and Taurus, the Bull. All have one or more first- and/or second-magnitude stars.

The summer sky has the Summer Triangle, and autumn the Great Square. The winter sky has a Winter Circle. The curved figure is formed by connecting seven outstanding stars with a curved line: **Capella** (kuh-PELL-uh), Castor, Pollux, **Procyon** (PRO-see-ahn), Sirius, **Rigel** (RYE-jul), and Aldebaran. Using the star map shown, find the Winter Circle by facing east and

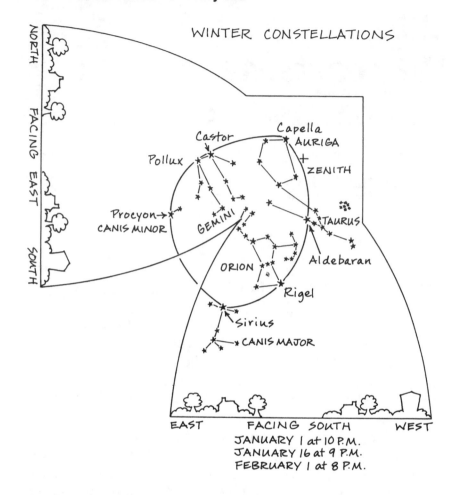

WINTER CONSTELLATIONS

EAST   FACING SOUTH   WEST
JANUARY 1 at 10 P.M.
JANUARY 16 at 9 P.M.
FEBRUARY 1 at 8 P.M.

looking near the zenith for the bright star Capella in Auriga. Follow a curved line southeast through Castor and Pollux in Gemini, to Procyon in Canis Minor, and south to Sirus in Canis Major low in the southeast. Facing south, look northwest to Rigel in Orion, to Aldebaran in Taurus, and north back to Capella.

Let's Think It Through

Study the winter constellations star map shown earlier for January 1 at 10 P.M. and the following imaginary figure representing a winter constellation to answer the following:

1. What is the name of the figure?

2. On the diagram below, is the figure in #1 located at position A, B, C, or D around the zenith?

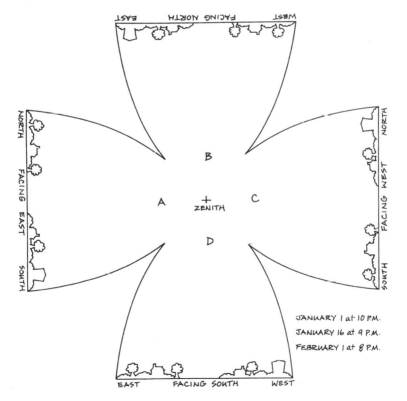

Answers

1. *Think!*

   • The figure shows a charging bull.

   • What star group represents a bull?

     The figure is Taurus.

2. *Think!*

   • For the dates shown, Taurus is in the southern sky near the zenith.

     Position D is the location of Taurus.

Exercises

Compare the stars in the diagrams of the constellation figures with those on the winter constellations star map shown earlier to answer the following:

1. Where is figure A located on January 1 at 10 P.M.?

2. Which figure represents Canis Minor?

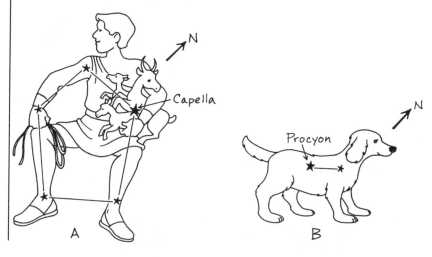

Activity: TWINKLING STARS

Purpose   To simulate twinkling stars.

Materials   2-quart (2-liter) glass bowl
tap water
small mirror that fits in the bottom of the bowl
flashlight

Procedure

1. Fill the bowl about three-fourths full with water.

2. Lay the mirror faceup in the bottom of the bowl of water.

3. Turn on the flashlight and darken the room.

4. Holding the flashlight at an angle about 6 inches (15 cm) above the bowl, move the flashlight as needed so that the light reflecting from the mirror hits a nearby wall.

5. Observe any motion of the light reflected on the wall.

6. Gently tap the surface of the water with your finger.

7. Again, observe the light reflected on the wall.

Results   There is little to no motion of the light reflecting from the mirror in still water. The reflected light passing through the moving water shimmers on the wall.

Why?   The reflected light rays are refracted as they leave the water. Different depths of water cause the refracted light to strike the wall in different places. The up-and-down movement of the water causes the depth of the water to vary and the reflected light to jump around. Light is affected by a material's thickness, which can be the material's depth or the **density** (how close together the particles in a material are) of the particles making up the material.

To an observer on Earth, light from distant stars also appears to jump around or twinkle because it refracts differently as it moves through different densities of air in Earth's atmosphere. Air has different densities because it is in constant motion. Warm air rises and expands, and cold air sinks and contracts. The density of warm air is less than the density of cold air. As starlight passes through the moving air, it refracts to differing degrees depending on the air's density. This change in direction of refracted light makes a star appear to change in brightness, or to twinkle. The twinkling or change in brightness is called **scintillation.**

All stars twinkle, some more than others. Sirius, in Canis Major, the brightest star in the sky after the Sun, twinkles more than any other star. Stars twinkle more near the horizon than high in the sky.

Solutions to Exercises

1. *Think!*

   • What is the name of the pentagon-shaped constellation represented in figure A? Auriga.

   • Where is Auriga located on the star map for January 1 at 10 P.M.?

     Facing east, Figure A, Auriga, is located near the zenith.

2. *Think!*

   • Canis Minor means "little dog."

   • Which figures represent dogs? B and D.

   • The star in Canis Minor is Procyon.

     Figure B is Canis Minor.

23
Winter Colors

Determining Star Types in Winter Constellations

What You Need to Know

The stars of the winter constellations, as well as constellations of other seasons, vary in color. Winter constellations have more bright stars than do some seasons. Cloudless winter nights offer hardy stargazers a breathtaking view of the sky's shimmering jewels. Although all stars have some color, most stars appear white to the naked eye. This is because your eye is not sensitive to color at the low light level of most stars. You can however, see the color of first-magnitude or brighter stars. Star colors of red, orange, yellow, white, and blue-white are more noticeable through a telescope or binoculars.

All visible stars are generally similar in composition. They are made mostly of hydrogen and helium. Since they are roughly uniform in composition, difference in color is a result of differences in their surface temperatures. When any object is hot enough, it gives off light. While an object red hot is too hot to touch, it is cool in comparison to something white hot. Blue hot is even hotter than white hot.

An astronomer's most important instrument, besides the telescope, is the **spectroscope.** This instrument is used to separate starlight into a band of colors called a **spectrum.** The spectra of stars vary with temperature. Hot stars have a different spectrum from that of cooler stars.

Stars are grouped according to their various types of spectrum. Stars are classed by seven spectral types, and a letter is assigned to each type. In order of decreasing surface temperature, the order of these letters is O B A F G K M. The famous **mnemonic** (memory device) used to remember these letters in order is "Oh, Be A Fine Girl (Guy), Kiss Me."

The chart lists spectral types, the approximate temperature range of each type, and the basic color of stars for each type. Note that different temperatures have different colors. The hotter temperatures produce blue-white starlight, and the cooler ones, red.

SPECTRAL TYPES

Type	Temperature (in °F [°C])	Color
O	>54,000 (30,000)	blue
B	18,000–54,000 (10,000–30,000)	blue
A	13,000–18,000 (7,500–10,000)	blue-white
F	10,800–13,000 (6,000–7,500)	white
G	8,100–10,800 (4,500–6,000)	yellow
K	6,300–8,100 (3,500–4,500)	orange
M	4,500–6,300 (2,500–3,500)	orange-red

Let's Think It Through

Use the Spectral Types chart and the diagram of Gemini on the next page to answer the following:

1. How many of the labeled stars are yellow?

2. Which are the coolest stars?

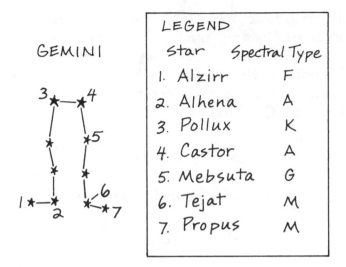

GEMINI

LEGEND

Star	Spectral Type
1. Alzirr	F
2. Alhena	A
3. Pollux	K
4. Castor	A
5. Mebsuta	G
6. Tejat	M
7. Propus	M

Answers

1.   *Think!*

- What spectral type is yellow? G.
- Which stars are type G? One star is type G, Mebsuta.

  There is one yellow star in the diagram of Gemini.

2.   *Think!*

- Which spectral type is the coolest? M.
- What are the names of the type M stars?

  Propus and Tejat are the coolest stars in the diagram of Gemini.

Exercises

Use the Spectral Types chart and the Winter Circle diagram to answer the following. (See chapter 22 for more information about the Winter Circle.)

1. How many stars are hotter than 13,000°F (7,500°C)?

2. Which constellation has the hottest star in the Winter Circle?

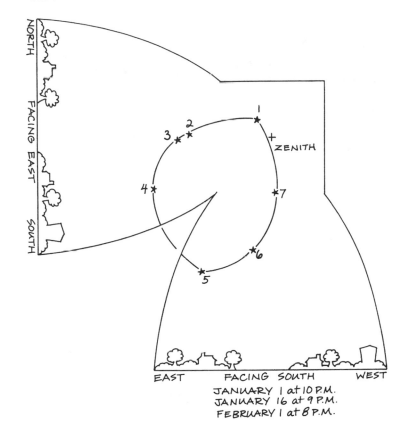

NORTH

FACING EAST

SOUTH

ZENITH

EAST   FACING SOUTH   WEST

JANUARY 1 at 10 P.M.
JANUARY 16 at 9 P.M.
FEBRUARY 1 at 8 P.M.

LEGEND		
Star	Constellation	Spectral Type
1. Capella	AURIGA	G
2. Castor	GEMINI	A
3. Pollux	GEMINI	K
4. Procyon	CANIS MINOR	F
5. Sirius	CANIS MAJOR	A
6. Rigel	ORION	B
7. Aldebaran	TAURUS	K

Activity: LIGHT SEPARATOR

Purpose To model how astronomers study the makeup of stars.

Materials compact disc (CD)

Procedure

CAUTION: Never look directly at the Sun, because doing so can damage your eyes.

1. Hold the compact disc so that sunlight coming through a window hits its shiny side.

2. Move the disc back and forth several times.

3. Observe the color patterns of the disc.

Results Bands of color are seen on the disc.

Why? The disc behaves like a spectroscope, which separates visible light into a spectrum. The colors on the disc appear to be a **continuous spectrum,** which means its colors are arranged in continuous order. The order of the colors seen are red, orange, yellow, green, blue, indigo, and violet. With a more precise instrument, such as a spectroscope, the Sun's spectrum is seen as a **dark-line spectrum** (a continuous spectrum crossed by dark lines). The placement of the dark lines gives astronomers clues they use to discover the types of **elements** (substances made of chemically identical particles) that make up the Sun or any star observed through a spectroscope.

Solutions to Exercises

1. *Think!*

    • Which spectral types are hotter than 13,000°F (7,500°C)? O, B, and A.

    • Which stars in the Winter Circle are type O, B, or A? There are no type O stars. Rigel is type B; Castor and Sirius are type A.

    There are three stars in the Winter Circle hotter than 13,000°F (7,500°C): Rigel, Castor, and Sirius.

2. *Think!*

    • Type O is the hottest. Are there any type O stars? No.

    • Type B is the second hottest. Are there any type B stars? Yes, Rigel.

    • What constellation is Rigel in?

    Orion has the hottest star in the Winter Circle.

24
The Hunter
Locating the Constellation Orion

What You Need to Know

Orion, the Hunter, is the most magnificent and outstanding constellation in the winter sky. Three equally bright stars in a row form Orion's Belt. The star farthest east is **Alnitak** (AL-nih-tock) at Orion's right side. The middle star is **Alnilam** (AL-nih-lahm), and the star farthest west is **Mintaka** (min-TOCK-uh) at Orion's left side. A dark nebula in the shape of a horse's head, and thus called the Horsehead Nebula, is not shown but is located near Alnitak.

Hanging from Orion's star-studded belt are dim stars forming a sword. Halfway down the blade is a fuzzy blur, the Orion Nebula. With a telescope, four glittering stars called the trapezium (truh-PEE-zee-um) can be seen in this emission nebula. (See chapter 13, "The Teapot," for more information about emission nebulae.) Below the belt are stars forming Orion's right and left knees. **Saiph** (SYFE) marks the position of the right knee, and Rigel, the left knee. Rigel is one of the sky's brightest stars.

To the east, at Orion's right shoulder, is the red star **Betelgeuse** (BEE-tul-joos). It is easy to remember a star called "Beetle Juice," and since it is also one of the sky's brightest stars, it's very easy to find. To the west, at Orion's left shoulder, is the star **Bellatrix** (be-LAY-triks). Above and between his shoulders is a group of three dim stars forming part of his head or neck.

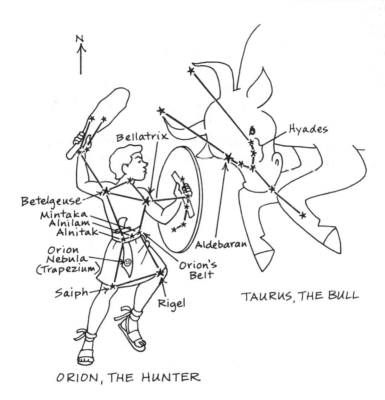

ORION, THE HUNTER

Orion is imagined as having a club raised high over his head in his right hand and a shield raised in his left hand to ward off an attack by Taurus, the Bull. One of the bull's eyes is marked by the bright orange star Aldebaran.

Using the star map, locate Orion by facing south and finding the three bright stars of Orion's Belt midway between the southern horizon and the zenith. Above the belt toward the west is Bellatrix. A line drawn northwest from Bellatrix points to Aldebaran, in Taurus. West of Aldebaran is Hyades (HIA-deez), an **open star cluster** (loose clusters of stars that contain at most a few thousand stars and sometimes less than twenty) of about 200 stars. The brightest of these are visible to the naked eye as the letter V that forms the face of the bull. (Aldebaran is not part of Hyades.) Orion has been described as distracting the bull from a group of girls northwest of the bull, called the

Pleiades (PLEE-uh-deez), the Seven Sisters. The Pleiades is one of the most famous open star clusters. This twinkling group of stars is part of Taurus and is found by continuing the line from Bellatrix in Orion through Aldebaran in Taurus. In a clear, dark sky, anyone with normal eyesight can usually make out at least seven separate stars in the Pleiades, hence the name Seven Sisters. One story goes that Native Americans tested warriors' eyesight by seeing how many stars of the Pleiades they could count. The actual number of stars in the cluster is around 400.

As a hunter, Orion has two hunting dogs, Canis Major, the Great Dog, and Canis Minor, the Little Dog. Canis Major can be located by following a line along Orion's belt southeast to Sirius in Canis Major, the brightest star in the sky (magnitude −1.5). Sirius is commonly known as the Dog Star. You might imagine this star as a jewel on the dog's collar.

Northeast of Sirius is Canis Minor. At best, only two stars are generally seen in this constellation. The brightest are Procyon, with a magnitude of 0.4, and **Gomeisa** (go-MEE-suh), with a magnitude of 2.9.

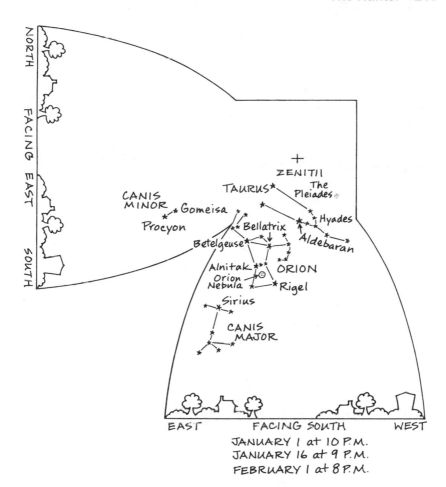

JANUARY 1 at 10 P.M.
JANUARY 16 at 9 P.M.
FEBRUARY 1 at 8 P.M.

Let's Think It Through

Study the constellation and select the diagram—A, B, C, or D—that represents the part of Orion's body or clothing marked by stars 1, 2, and 3.

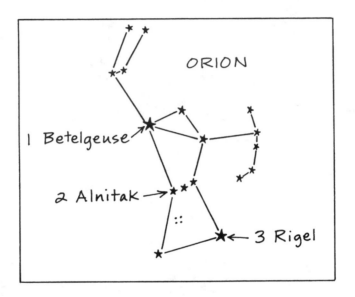

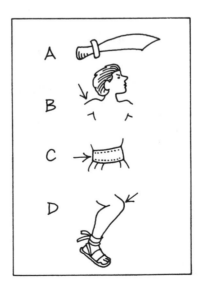

Answers

1. *Think!*

   • Star 1, Betelgeuse, marks Orion's right shoulder.

   Diagram B represents a right shoulder, marked by Betelgeuse, star 1.

2. *Think!*

   • Star 2, Alnitak, marks part of Orion's Belt.

   Diagram C represents a belt, marked by Alnitak, star 2.

3. *Think!*

   • Star 3, Rigel, marks Orion's left knee.

   Diagram D represents a left knee, marked by Rigel, star 3.

Exercises

Study the star map for January 1 at 10 P.M. and the following imaginary figures—A and B—representing constellations near the constellation Orion to answer the following:

1. What is the constellation name of each figure?

2. On the star map, is figure B located at position 1, 2, or 3 around Orion?

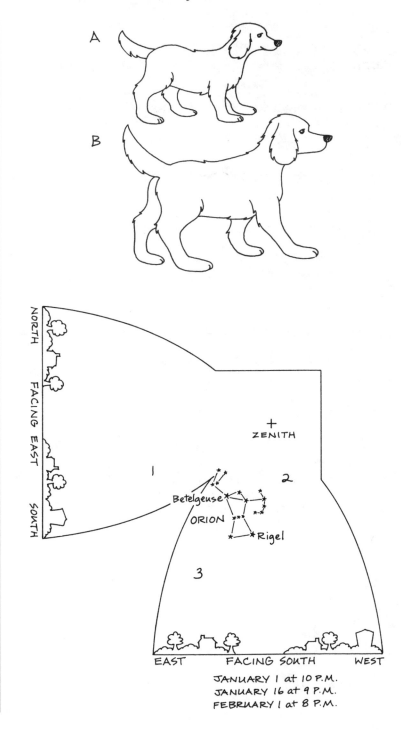

A

B

NORTH

FACING EAST

SOUTH

+
ZENITH

1

2

Betelgeuse

ORION

Rigel

3

EAST   FACING SOUTH   WEST

JANUARY 1 at 10 P.M.
JANUARY 16 at 9 P.M.
FEBRUARY 1 at 8 P.M.

Activity: SILHOUETTE

Purpose   To simulate a dark nebula.

Materials   pencil
index card
scissors
transparent tape
table lamp
sheet of typing paper

Procedure

1. Draw the profile of the horse's head on the index card.

2. Cut out the drawing and tape it to the pencil so that the ears of the horse point toward the pencil eraser.

3. Turn the lamp on and hold the sheet of paper about 12 inches (30 cm) from the lamp.

4. Place the pencil about 2 inches (5 cm) from the paper between the paper and the lamp.

5. Look at the image on the paper.

Results   A dark shape of the horse's head is seen on the paper.

Why?   A nebula is a vast cloud of interstellar dust and gas in space. Dark nebulae, like the cutout of the horse's head, absorb or scatter light, creating a dark **silhouette** (a dark shape set against a light background). The Horsehead Nebula, located near Alnitak in Orion's Belt, is an example of a dark nebula. It gets its name from the horse-head shape of its silhouette.

Solutions to Exercises

1a. *Think!*

- Figure A is a small dog.

- What star group represents a small dog?

  Figure A is Canis Minor.

b. *Think!*

- Figure B is a large dog.
- What star group represents a large dog?

  Figure B is Canis Major.

2. *Think!*

- Canis Major is below and to the east of Orion.

  Position 3 is the location of Canis Major.

Star Maps of the Seasons

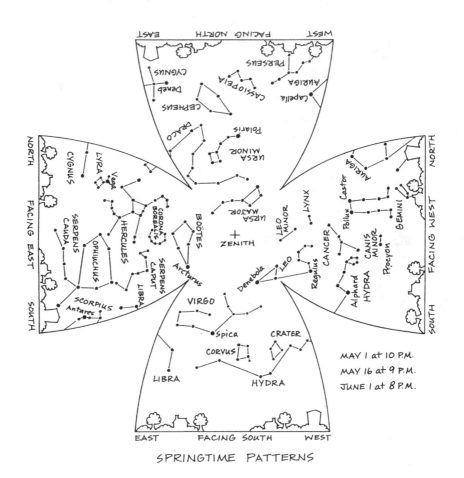

MAY 1 at 10 P.M.
MAY 16 at 9 P.M.
JUNE 1 at 8 P.M.

SPRINGTIME PATTERNS

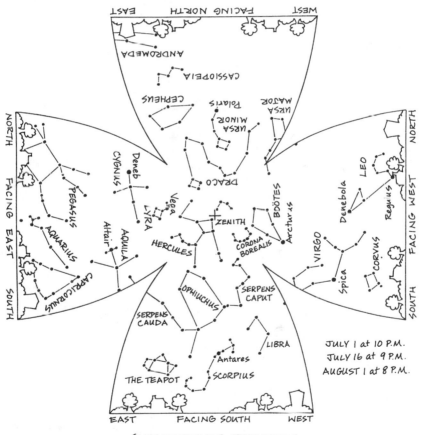

SUMMERTIME PATTERNS

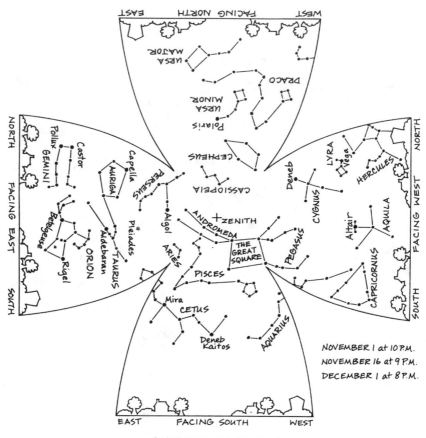

NOVEMBER 1 at 10 P.M.
NOVEMBER 16 at 9 P.M.
DECEMBER 1 at 8 P.M.

AUTUMN PATTERNS

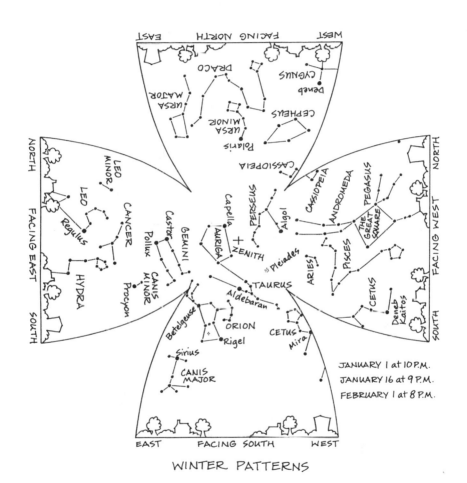

WINTER PATTERNS

Appendix B
List of Constellations

Name	Pronunciation
Andromeda, the Princess	an-DRAH-muh-duh
Aquarius, the Water Bearer	uh-KWAIR-ee-us
Aquila, the Eagle	A-kwuh-luh
Aries, the Ram	AIR-eez
Auriga, the Charioteer	aw-RYE-guh
Boötes, the Herdsman	boh-OH-teez
Cancer, the Crab	KAN-sur
Canis Major, the Great Dog	KAY-nus MAY-jur
Canis Minor, the Little Dog	KAY-nus MY-nur
Capricornus, the Sea Goat	ka-prih-KOR-nus
Cassiopeia, the Queen	kas-ee-oh-PEE-uh
Cepheus, the King	SEE-fyus
Cetus, the Whale	SEE-tus
Corona Australis, the Southern Cross	kuh-ROH-nuh aw-STRAY-lus
Corona Borealis, the Northern Cross	kuh-ROH-nuh bor-ee-A-lus
Corvus, the Crow	KOR-vus
Cygnus, the Swan	SIG-nus
Draco, the Dragon	DRAY-koh
Gemini, the Twins	JEH-muh-nye
Hercules, the Kneeler	HUR-kyoo-leez
Hydra, the Sea Monster	HYE-druh

Name	Pronunciation
Leo, the Lion	LEE-oh
Libra, the Scales	LEE-bruh
Lyra, the Lyre	LYE-ruh
Norma, the Level	NOR-muh
Ophiuchus, the Serpent Bearer	oh-fee-YOO-kus
Orion, the Hunter	uh-RYE-un
Pegasus, the Winged Horse	PEH-guh-sus
Perseus, the Hero	PUR-sus
Pisces, the Fish	PYE-seez
Sagittarius, the Archer or the Teapot	sa-juh-TAIR-ee-us
Scorpius, the Scorpion	SKOR-pee-us
Serpens Caput, Head of the Snake	SUR-penz KAH-put
Serpens Cauda, Tail of the Snake	SUR-penz COW-duh
Taurus, the Bull	TOR-us
Tucana, the Toucan	too-KAN-uh
Ursa Major, the Great Bear or the Big Dipper	UR-suh MAY-jur
Ursa Minor, the Little Bear or the Little Dipper	UR-suh MY-nur
Virgo, the Maiden	VUR-go

Appendix C

List of Stars

Name	Pronunciation	Constellation
Alcor	AL-kor	Ursa Major
Aldebaran	al-DEH-buh-run	Taurus
Algenib	al-JEE-nib	Pegasus
Algol	AL-gawl	Perseus
Alnilam	AL-nih-lahm	Orion
Alnitak	AL-nih-tock	Orion
Alphard	AL-fard	Hydra
Alpheratz	al-FEE-rats	Andromeda
Alrisha	al-RISH-uh	Pisces
Altair	al-TYRE	Aquila
Antares	an-TAIR-eez	Scorpius
Arcturus	ark-TUR-us	Boötes
Bellatrix	be-LAY-triks	Orion
Betelgeuse	BEE-tul-joos	Orion
Capella	kuh-PELL-uh	Auriga
Caph	KAF	Cassiopeia
Castor	KAS-tur	Gemini
Chi	KYE	Cassiopeia
Delta Cephei	DEL-tuh SEH-fee-eye	Cepheus
Deneb	DEH-neb	Cygnus
Deneb Kaitos	DEH-neb KAY-tos	Cetus
Denebola	duh-NEB-uh-luh	Leo
Dubhe	DOO-bee	Ursa Major
El Nath	el NATH	Taurus

Name	Pronunciation	Constellation
Er Rai	ehr RYE	Cepheus
Gomeisa	go-MEE-suh	Canis Minor
Hamal	huh-MAHL	Aries
Markab	MAR-kab	Pegasus
Megrez	MEH-grez	Ursa Major
Merak	MEE-rak	Ursa Major
Mesarthim	MEZ-ar-thim	Aries
Mintaka	min-TOCK-uh	Orion
Mira	MY-ruh	Cetus
Mirfak	MUR-fak	Perseus
Mizar	MEE-zar	Ursa Major
Phecda	FEK-duh	Ursa Major
Polaris	puh-LAIR-us	Ursa Minor
Pollux	PAH-luks	Gemini
Procyon	PRO-see-ahn	Canis Minor
Rasalgethi	raz-ul-GEE-thee	Hercules
Regulus	REH-gyuh-lus	Leo
Rigel	RYE-jul	Orion
Saiph	SYFE	Orion
Scheat	SHEE-at	Pegasus
Shaula	SHOW-luh	Scorpius
Sheratan	SHER-uh-tun	Aries
Sirius	SIHR-ee-us	Canis Major
Spica	SPY-kuh	Virgo
Thuban	THOO-ban	Draco
Vega	VEE-guh	Lyra

Glossary

absolute magnitude: A measure of luminosity. A measure of the brightness of a star if it were placed at a distance of 32.6 light-years from Earth.

air pressure: The force air puts on an area.

altitude: The height of an object, measured in degrees above the horizon.

apparent brightness: How bright a celestial object appears to be as observed from Earth.

apparent magnitude: The measure of a celestial object's apparent brightness.

apparent magnitude scale: A list of apparent magnitudes, in which lower magnitude numbers indicate brighter objects.

asterism: A group of stars with a shape within a constellation.

astrolabe: An instrument used to measure the altitude of a celestial object.

astrology: A pseudoscience; a belief that the Sun, stars, planets, and the Moon affect people's lives.

astronomers: Scientists who study the stars and other celestial bodies.

atoms: The smallest building blocks of matter.

autumnal equinox: The position of the sun on about September 23, when it crosses the celestial equator and heads south; also called the fall equinox.

axis: An imaginary line through the center of an object.

azimuth: The distance of an object in degrees clockwise around the horizon from north.

binary star: Double stars bound by their mutual gravity and revolving around a common point.

celestial: Having to do with the sky.

celestial bodies: Things, such as stars, suns, moons, and planets, in the sky.

celestial equator: An imaginary line at 0° declination that circles the celestial sphere at the same distance north and south of the celestial poles; a great circle.

celestial globe: A model of the celestial sphere.

celestial meridian: An hour circle that passes through the zenith and the north and south endpoints of an observer's horizon.

celestial sphere: An imaginary sphere that has Earth at its center and all other celestial bodies stuck to its inside surface.

cepheid: A pulsating variable star that changes brightness in a predictable time period, such as the star Delta Cephei.

circumpolar constellation: A constellation that, when viewed from a specific location on Earth, is always above the horizon and near the celestial pole.

cluster: A group of a few to many thousands of stars held together by their gravity.

compass rose: An instrument used to measure the azimuth of a celestial object.

constellations: Groups of stars that appear to make patterns in the sky.

continuous spectrum: A spectrum that has colors arranged in continuous order.

contract: To move close together.

converge: To come together, as light rays passing through a convex lens converge at the focal point.

convex lens: A lens that is thicker in the center than at the edge and causes light passing through it to converge.

coordinates: Two numbers that mark the location of a place.

dark-line spectrum: A continuous spectrum crossed by dark lines.

dark nebula: A nebula that does not give off visible light and is so thick that it partially or completely blocks the light shining from the stars behind it.

declination: The position of a celestial body in degrees north or south of the celestial equator; imaginary lines that circle the celestial sphere parallel to the celestial equator and mark locations in degrees north and south of the celestial equator, which is at 0° declination.

dense: Having materials that are close together.

density: How close together the particles in a material are.

double star: Two stars that appear close together in the sky.

eclipse: To pass in front of and block the light of another body.

eclipsing binary: A binary star in which one star periodically moves in front of the other.

eclipsing variables: Variable stars that change in brightness because they are concealed by another star that is in the observer's line of vision and blocks the light of the star behind it for a period of time.

ecliptic: The Sun's apparent yearly path across the sky.

elements: Substances made of chemically identical particles.

emission nebula: A nebula that shines by its own light.

equator: An imaginary line at 0° latitude circling the center of Earth or the celestial sphere in an east-west direction; the starting point for measuring distances north or south on a map or globe; a great circle.

equilibrium: A state of balance in opposing forces.

eruptive variables: Variable stars that change in brightness because they experience explosions.

expand: To spread out.

eyepiece: The lens of binoculars or a telescope that is closest to the eye and magnifies the image formed by the objective lens.

fall equinox: See **autumnal equinox.**

focal point: The place where refracted light rays converge.

galaxy: An enormous group of stars, dust, and gas held together by the force of gravity. Comes from Greek word for milk, *gala*.

globular cluster: Cluster of several tens of thousands to maybe 1 million stars.

gravity: The force of attraction between celestial bodies that pulls them toward each other.

great circle: An imaginary circle on a sphere with the center point of the circle and the center point of the sphere being the same.

horizon: A line where the sky seems to meet Earth.

hour circle: A great circle passing through the north and south poles on the celestial sphere; half of such a circle from pole to pole is used to determine right ascension of a celestial body.

interstellar dust: Microscopic particles thought to be mainly of carbon and/or silicates between celestial bodies.

interstellar material: Material between celestial bodies.

irregular pulsating variables: Pulsating variables that don't have a regular time pattern for brightness changes.

lagoon: A large body of water.

latitude lines: Imaginary lines that circle Earth parallel to its equator and mark locations in degrees north and south of the equator, which is at 0° latitude.

light-year: A measure of distance equal to about 5.9 trillion miles (9.4 trillion km) in space; 1 light-year equals the distance that light, at a speed of 186,000 miles (300,000 km) per second, travels in 1 year.

longitude lines: Imaginary lines that run from the North Pole to the South Pole and mark locations in degrees east and west of the prime meridian, which is at 0° longitude.

luminosity: The quantity of light given off in a given time.

luminous: Shining by its own light.

magnifies: Makes larger.

Milky Way: The hazy band of starlight visible across the night sky; the starlight seen by an observer on Earth looking through the Milky Way Galaxy toward the rim of the galaxy.

Milky Way Galaxy: The galaxy that is made up of the Sun, all the planets of our solar system, and more than 100 billion stars, including those that are close enough to see with the naked eye.

mnemonic: A memory device.

moon: A small celestial body that revolves around a planet; (capital *M*) the Earth's moon.

nebula (plural **nebulae**): A cloud of interstellar dust and gas spread across many millions of miles (kilometers) in space.

night vision: The ability to see in the dark.

north celestial pole: The point on the celestial sphere directly above the North Pole of Earth.

northern circumpolar constellations: Constellations that never set but move around Polaris in a circular path above the horizon.

Northern Hemisphere: The region of Earth north of the equator.

North Pole: The northernmost point on Earth.

North Star: The star closest to the point on the celestial sphere above the North Pole, which at present is Polaris.

nova (plural **novae**):   A type of variable star whose outer layer explodes so that the star suddenly becomes bright enough to see, then after a period of time fades out of sight again.

nuclear fusion: The joining of two nuclei to form one nucleus, as when hydrogen in the center of most stars fuses to form helium, releasing great amounts of light and heat.

nucleus (plural **nuclei**):   The center of an atom.

objective lens: The convex lens at the end of a telescope, which gathers light rays and converges them to a focal point.

open star cluster: A loose cluster of stars that contains at most a few thousand stars and sometimes less than twenty.

optical double: Two stars that only appear to be very close together but are far apart and have no relationship to each other.

optical illusion: A false mental image.

orbit: The path of one celestial body around another.

parallax: The apparent shift in the position of an object against a distant background when viewed from different places.

parallels: See **latitude lines.**

pentagon: Five-sided figure.

planet: A large celestial body that revolves around a sun.

precession: The change in direction of Earth's axis.

primary star: The brighter of the two stars in a binary.

prime meridian: An imaginary line at 0° longitude that runs from pole to pole through Greenwich, England.

pseudoscience: A set of beliefs pretending to be scientific but not based on scientific principles.

pulsating variables: Stars that change in brightness due to periodic contraction and expansion of their outer layers.

reflect: To bounce back, as light off an object.

refract: To bend, as light rays.

refractive telescope: A telescope with two lenses, an objective lens and an eyepiece.

revolve: To move around a central point, as Earth moves around the Sun.

right ascension: The position of a celestial body in hours (where 1 hour equals 15°) east from the vernal equinox at 0^h to the place where the celestial body's hour circle crosses the celestial equator.

rotate: To spin on an axis.

scintillation: The twinkling or change in brightness of stars.

secondary star: The fainter of the two stars in a binary.

silhouette: A dark shape set against a light background.

solar system: A group of celestial bodies traveling around a sun.

south celestial pole: The southernmost point on the celestial sphere, directly below Earth's South Pole.

Southern Hemisphere: The region of Earth south of the equator.

South Pole: The southernmost point on Earth.

spectroscope: An instrument used by astronomers to separate starlight to study the spectra of stars.

spectrum (plural **spectra**):   A band of colors produced when visible light is separated.

spiral galaxy: A flat, disklike galaxy with a bright, dense center and radiating arms of stars, planets, and other celestial bodies.

spring equinox: See **vernal equinox.**

stars: Luminous bodies outside our solar system that are made mostly of hydrogen and helium gases and produce light as a result of nuclear fusion.

stellar parallax: The parallax of a star.

summer solstice: The position of the Sun on about June 21, when it is farthest north of the celestial equator.

Sun: A star in the center of a solar system; the nearest star to Earth.

telescope: An instrument that makes far-off objects appear to be closer and larger.

terrestrial globe: A model of Earth.

transparent: Capable of being passed straight through by light.

variable star: A single star that changes in brightness over time. Other changes over time may be in size, brightness, and color. The three major groups are explosive, eclipsing, and pulsating variables.

vernal equinox: The position of the Sun on about March 21, when it crosses the celestial equator and heads north; also called the spring equinox.

visual binary: A binary star whose stars are far enough apart to be seen separately with the naked eye or with binoculars or a telescope.

winter solstice: The position of the Sun on about December 21, when it is farthest south of the celestial equator.

zenith: The point on the celestial sphere directly above an observer or object.

zodiac: A narrow zone on either side of the ecliptic.

zodiac constellations: The constellations within the zodiac.

Index